Facilitator Notes for Investigations into Economic Class in America

Philip E. DeVol
Karla M. Krodel

Facilitator Notes for Investigations into Economic Class in America
Philip E. DeVol and Karla M. Krodel
193 pp.
Works Cited pp. 173–178

Published by aha! Process, Inc.

ISBN 13: 978-1-934583-47-0
ISBN 10: 1-934583-47-2

Copy editing by Dan Shenk and Jesse Conrad
Book design by Paula Nicolella
Cover design by Naylor Design

Printed in the United States of America

Table of Contents

Acknowledgments

This work would not exist without the insights and experience of Ruby Payne. Her groundbreaking book *A Framework for Understanding Poverty* has sparked many applications in the practice of improving education for students of all ages. All the staff persons of aha! Process, Inc. provide tremendous support, but special thanks go to Peg Conrad, vice president of Publications, and Bethanie Tucker. Our gratitude also goes to Dan Shenk and Jesse Conrad for their editing expertise, as well as to Paula Nicolella for her outstanding work designing the book.

This book benefited greatly from the wisdom and insights from people who completed *Getting Ahead in a Just-Gettin'-By World* (the original version of this work) and those who reviewed content and activities contained in this book. They include co-facilitators Janae Books, Carlos Guajardo, Sonia Holycross, Yolanda Reed, and Terrell Wesley, along with Rebecca Banks, Brandy Bates, Alberta Bevly, Lisa Carlock, Remona Gordon, Jacqueline Hall, Tanavia Hodges, Malcom Horton, Karen Jones, Cathy Lenoir, Gracie Rollins, Maryann Rought, Lawarnda Smith, and Suzie Wright (who also helped in the design of the book).

In addition, several talented facilitators contributed their ideas and support, including Karen Kessler, Patricia Matthews, Kathy McPherson, Lenore Moore, and Gale Vaughn. Thank you for "keeping it real."

There are many "communities of practice" across North America using the concepts in Phil DeVol's books through Bridges Steering Committees and Move the Mountain's Circles™ Campaign. Thanks to Scott Miller, Vikki Boatman, Marian Brannon, Marlo Fox, Catherine Iannello, Clay Randall, Laura Solano, Lisa Stoddard, Judith Valade, Karin Van Zant, Tay Waltenbaugh, Dee Washington, and Lisa Yaeger. Thank you for sharing your insights and confirming the need for this work.

There are many people from colleges, universities, and trade schools who helped us with this work. Some became early adopters of Getting Ahead with postsecondary students and shared results, needs, and ideas; some reviewed and advised us about these books; and some contributed content in their areas of practice. Your expertise is much appreciated, and we hope you find it has been well used here. Thank you to Vicki Thompson and Linda Reader of Trumbull Career and Technical Center in Champion, Ohio, the first school we know of that incorporated the *Getting Ahead* workbook into an accredited educational program (licensed practical nursing); Bonnie Bazata, executive director of St. Joseph County Bridges Out of Poverty Initiative, South Bend Indiana; Gale Vaughn, facilitator and assistant director of Admissions at Ivy Tech,

South Bend, Indiana, the first college-based Getting Ahead program we are aware of; and Diane Kloss, Sondra O'Donnell, and Pauline Tressler at Kent State University, Columbiana, Ohio, campuses, for pioneering Getting Ahead in career pathway and workforce initiatives.

The following scholars and practitioners consulted with us on aspects of the book as it was developed, and we are indebted to you: Bill Border, Sherri Harper-Woods, Henry Ingle, Cryshanna Jackson, Susan Jakes, Sherry Linkon, Guy Shebat, and Rebecca Wheeler.

A special thanks to our thoughtful reviewers whose insights and suggestions greatly improved this work and validated it: Karen Becker, reading and study skills coordinator and adjunct instructor at Youngstown (Ohio) State University; Virginia Calvin, chancellor, Ivy Tech Community College North Central (Indiana); Edward Carmien, associate professor of English, Mercer County (New Jersey) Community College; Lisa Horan, director, Center for Community Building to End Poverty, Lewiston, Idaho; Alicia Liss, former vice president, Warren County (New Jersey) Community College, director, College Circles Program, and Getting Ahead instructor, Sussex County (New Jersey) Community College; Karon J. Rosa, program director, Arkansas Department of Higher Education; Victoria Van Steenhouse, associate professor emeritus, Applied Behavioral Studies, Delta College, University Center, Michigan; and Monieca West, director, Carl D. Perkins CTE Post Secondary Program, Arkansas Department of Higher Education.

And finally, heartfelt thanks to Susan DeVol and Craig Paulenich, our respective spouses, whose unfailing love and support over the last two years have made this work possible.

A Message from the Authors

Education That Transforms

Investigations into Economic Class in America opens doors to rich areas of intellectual thought and academic content related to the history of class, causes of poverty, change theory, language development, and associated arts and literature. This balance of intellectual development based on the study of economic class and personal self-discovery, fostered by the relevance of the content, fits the needs of students in a variety of postsecondary institutions. In the foreword to *Pedagogy of the Oppressed,* Richard Shaull writes:

> There is no such thing as a *neutral* educational process. Education either functions as an instrument that is used to facilitate the integration of the younger generation into the logic of the present system and bring about conformity to it, *or* **education becomes "the practice of freedom," the means by which men and women deal critically and creatively with reality and discover how to participate in the transformation of their world.** (Freire, 1999, p. 16)

The student workbook is unique in that it (1) both examines and begins to address the realities of political/economic systems that contribute to poverty and (2) trusts the students to analyze their situation, to solve problems, and to transform their world. The educational process underlying this workbook can lead to individual transformations. This approach is fundamentally different from most other entry-level strategies, and we believe that these differences are crucial.

The process of studying economic class and the hidden rules of class illuminates the discrepancy between life as it is now and what it might be in the future—and this motivates individuals toward personal change. We must be cognizant of the nature of that change. The goal is for that personal change to be driven by self-awareness, informed by the theories of economic class, and free from the agenda of other people.

Personal change becomes "the practice of freedom." This workbook will help you (the facilitator) illustrate the differences between the self-empowerment of making informed choices to achieve economic stability and the essentially passive resignation of doing what others think one should do or ought to do. Thus this is not about "training," "soft skills," or "assimilation." Moving from poverty to economic stability and prosperity doesn't require conformity to the system or that one embrace any particular ideology or political philosophy—or strive or want to become middle class. One can choose to use knowledge about the "hidden rules" of economic classes and how to build resources without losing touch with community, family, or personal identity. Having more stability, choice, and power allows for different approaches to *shape one's own reality.*

This educational process can transform students from feelings of helplessness about their situation to becoming an active driving force in their own future, including becoming visible and effective in society. Generally speaking, people from poverty are not present when decisions that affect their lives are made. They are invisible. Their lives are interpreted, and assumptions are made by others, such as middle-class educators and policymakers from wealth, most of whom have little or no firsthand experience with poverty. Equipped with the information from this course, students can come to the table as problem solvers, advisers, and informed decision makers. Their visibility and civic engagement can have a positive impact on college campuses and on many of the conditions that contribute to poverty in their community. Jane Vella, author of *Learning to Listen, Learning to Teach* (2002), puts it this way:

> When we work diligently to design learning tasks that are in simple and sound sequence and that reinforce learning, we address the disparity in political power more directly than if we preach loudly on social and economic injustice. These rather technical principles and practices—reinforcement and sequence—are tough to use. They demand attention and diligence to design. When you do that hard work, you are in fact addressing sociopolitical-economic inequalities. It is all of a piece. (pp. 13–14)

Faculty and staff may find involvement with this workbook to be a transformational experience as well. As we learn about economic class from our students' experience, we too will develop a better understanding of ourselves and have the opportunity, as Shaull says, to deal "critically and creatively with reality and discover how to participate in the transformation of [our] world." Within our institution the process creates the possibility of transformation or, at the least, change that incorporates multi-class perspectives and experiences to the benefit of all students.

An invitation: Please share how you use *Investigations into Economic Class in America,* your students' thoughts about these materials, your use of additional supplemental materials, and your insights and observations. We invite you to join, contribute to, and benefit from a community of practice through the *www.gettingaheadnetwork.com/college* website.

Philip E. DeVol
Karla M. Krodel

March 2010

I. Overview

Welcome!

Thank you for using *Investigations into Economic Class in America* as a student text. This workbook is designed to increase the retention and graduation rates of under-resourced college students. These solutions are grounded in the duality of two intertwined realities: (1) first-generation, low-income college students (as a group) fail to complete college programs at an unacceptably high rate and (2) most of our institutions too often fail in the mission to effectively educate and graduate them.

Economic Class as an Analytical Category

Economic class is a unique analytical category for understanding and addressing poverty. **We describe poverty as "the extent to which one does without resources" (Payne, 2005), as opposed to a level of income or wealth. We make a distinction in our definition of economic class by focusing on how the *economic environment* affects one's stability, access to power, and ability to make choices because *these are the issues most central to the success of students from under-resourced backgrounds.*** The lens of economic class can be used to understand income and wealth disparity, the economic environments in which people live, and the "hidden rules" that arise from those environments. Knowledge of the hidden rules can make it possible for people from different classes to overcome their own biases and build relationships of mutual respect across class lines.

We describe the economic environments of poverty, middle class, and wealth while fully cognizant that there are more than three *social* classes in North America. For example, there are the working class and the *nouveau riche,* the proletariat and the bourgeoisie, as well as the owners of the means of production. Paul Fussell (1983, p. 27) defines nine classes, while the marketing firm Claritas, Inc., has proprietary software that delineates more than 60 segments of U.S. society. Our intention is not to narrow the inquiry by de-emphasizing the effect of personal characteristics, available opportunity, and/or ability. Nor is the intent to condemn all aspects of life in poverty. There are distinct advantages to living in any economic class. In short, *Investigations* invites exploration without glamorizing and romanticizing or, on the other hand, vilifying and condemning any one "way of being."

Our approach to economic class provides a way for people of all races, classes, sectors, and political persuasions to come together at planning tables with a shared understanding of class as a key component in problem solving. It provides a perspective on the pronounced disparity in income and wealth we are experiencing. If we can agree on this and the process of change that underlies the work, it will allow us to be more consistent in the way we present the information, while nonetheless allowing considerable flexibility for incorporating additional content.

Understanding the Experience of Under-Resourced Students

College students from under-resourced environments are often "living life" at a level much more intense than that of their middle-class peers. They frequently work one or more jobs, manage household and childcare issues (their own children, siblings, or children of relatives), deal with unreliable transportation—and might also be coping with stressors ranging from neighborhood crime to poor health to disabilities. With respect to college success, they face particular challenges related to:

- Finding relevance in abstract information (education) as it relates to their concrete realities
- Understanding the hidden rules of economic class, including those peculiar to college
- "Code switching" between casual and formal register and the attendant language skills—vocabulary, discourse patterns, story structure, voice, and negotiation
- Social capital and relationships that support change—and provide (or link to) resources to meet goals
- Envisioning their own "future story" and creating and executing realistic plans to actualize it

Our educational institutions, heavily vested in the middle-class driving forces of education and achievement, are alien landscapes for most first-generation, low-income students who usually lack the intergenerational transfer of "college knowledge." Despite the increasingly diverse student body in most college and university settings (in terms of economic class, race, ethnicity, native language, etc.) we continue to function, by and large, as if students arrive equipped with knowledge of the rules within the culture of postsecondary education, with an assumption that they know how to navigate our institutions on our terms.

Investigations into Economic Class in America is designed to facilitate a process of change. The personal change experienced by students supports their academic success, retention, and ability to use higher levels of cognition. *Investigations* provides under-resourced students a safe space to analyze how poverty impacts them and their communities, as well the opportunity to explore economic realities. This is a starting point for developing higher levels of cognition and plans for transition. Considering the resources necessary for a full life (in Module 7) and the hidden rules of economic class (as described in Modules 5 and 6) students can evaluate themselves, choose language and behaviors, and make plans to build resources and economic stability.

Through the lens of economic class, students come to understand income and wealth disparity, the economic environments in which people live, and the hidden rules that arise from those environments. In partnership with individuals from middle class and wealth, students begin to solve community and systemic problems that contribute to the cycle of poverty. Working with others across societal strata, individuals begin to see how their biases get represented in institutional structures and policies, thereby leading to change (Payne, DeVol, & Smith, 2006). **People from different classes begin, together, to overcome their judgmental attitudes and build relationships of mutual respect.**

Investigations begins by using the knowledge about economic class that students bring to the table. Additional information about the causes of poverty (choices of the poor, community capital, exploitation, and political/economic structures) and the effects of poverty on individuals and society is introduced. **Using the lens of economic class, students and faculty develop a more broadly defined social and academic landscape within which to build knowledge, skills, relationships, and resources.** As a result, students increase their own self-awareness as they come to understand the larger socioeconomic and political context that affects individuals and communities. Tacit knowledge bases—including how to use hidden rules of poverty, middle class, and wealth, as well as how to build resources—are explored. The deeply personal relevance of the subject matter highlights the disparity between current reality and a new future story. **This fuels the motivation needed to actualize personal growth. *Investigations* then provides invitations and opportunities that put students in charge of their own learning and planning.** The group process develops positive peer support for change. This involvement in the learning process further motivates students—and supports college success and civic engagement within the (college) community and within social/political structures around them.

In most college courses about poverty, people in poverty are talked about as objects. In *Investigations,* students talk about their own reality in light of the concepts and ideas presented. There isn't "othering" of under-resourced students; rather, there's a co-investigative process with the facilitator. **For college students from under-resourced backgrounds, this personal insight can be transformational, empowering students to confront the real obstacles to college success.** By providing a framework for understanding the economic and societal experience of life in the United States, *Investigations* directly addresses that "differentness" many students feel—and empowers the students to take on the issues and challenges they experience.

Investigations catalyzes change, but change occurs over time and requires the long-term support and social capital mentioned above. Consider what will happen after the course to support the student. Will there be a second semester as part of a first-year experience? Can student services be intentionally organized to support students after the *Investigations* course? How can partners from the community become involved? Additional discussion about ongoing support and community partnerships appears in Section V. on Planning and Managing the Course.

How *Investigations* Came to Be

The process and some of the ideas contained in *Investigations into Economic Class in America* were originally developed in collaboration with several groups of adults from poverty in community settings. As an outgrowth of this investigation of poverty, and based upon extensive field research, the original workbook *Getting Ahead in a Just-Gettin'-By World: Building Your Resources for a Better Life* (DeVol, 2004) was developed for utilization by community organizations to equip people from generational poverty with tools essential for making the transition out of poverty. Since then, early adopters in postsecondary schools have used the workbook as part of a semester-long study process and found that it accelerated students' ability to reach college-level performance. Early data and anecdotal evidence reflect improved retention and completion rates compelling enough to warrant this revision of the text for the college-level audience.

When Using the Student Workbook

The processes underlying the workbook have had extensive field testing for five years in communities across North America. And although the workbook is designed with built-in flexibility, we've learned that any significant deviation from the core content and sequence generally backfires. For example, *Investigations* is not designed to be incorporated into an existing course or into a college orientation course: It is designed to *be* the course. Rather than trying to make it "fit" a predetermined curriculum, applicable pieces of that curriculum should be used to buttress *Investigations* instead. Similarly, the learning modules are necessarily intended to be studied in their entirety, as well as in the sequence that they are presented. Utilizing the workbook by following these methods has proved to be the most effective. Appendixes A and B provide the "30,000-foot view" of the modules and the sequenced learning processes, while Appendix F provides a Lesson Planner indicating core content areas and essential in-class discussions.

Facilitator Notes is intended to support your work with students. Experienced educators will likely be familiar with and already use many of the strategies and techniques that we present here. These suggestions are reminders that the success of students using the workbook hinges on a consistent pedagogical approach—that of sequenced, facilitated co-investigation.

A Continuum of Applications

- At one end of the continuum, *Investigations* is used as a non-credit "bridge" course as part of programs to prepare students for postsecondary education.
- At the other end of the continuum, *Investigations* is used as a *bona fide* credit-bearing course in such disciplines as sociology, political science, social work, health professions, and education.
- *Investigations* lends itself to being used as the context for other courses—such as for orientation courses, for teaching college success and study skills, or as the context for English composition assignments at the developmental or credit level.
- *Investigations* is being offered as the centerpiece of a learning community model that includes a developmental writing course, which uses a series of assignments that are coordinated with *Investigations*. Cohort programs include additional entry-level courses, such as Introduction to Sociology or U.S. Government, which allow students to see the interconnectedness of the courses required for degrees.

Sample course descriptions, syllabi, and schedules can be found in the appendixes. More detailed descriptions of these courses are available at *www.gettingaheadnetwork.com/college.*

Common First Impressions/Questions

- ***"Can a book this thin actually serve as a text for a college course?"*** *Investigations* is a framework that provides a conceptual model about economic class. A great deal of material will be provided by the students themselves during class discussions. The framework offers a new way to understand their experiences and perceptions. The expectation is that, if facilitators feel the need, they will offer supplemental content from their discipline and interest areas, and/or assignments based on additional readings. Sociology, psychology, economics, literature, philosophy, healthcare, human services, education, and other fields all connect well to *Investigations* and allow you to build on the materials presented.

- ***"Is it rigorous enough academically?"*** *Investigations* is used in a variety of settings requiring varying degrees of academic rigor. Our intention was to create materials and a process flexible enough for different needs. When it's used as a non-credit bridge or college prep course, the focus is on the personal processes within the workbook—and building personal resources. Overloading pre-college-level students with large numbers of reading and writing assignments may be counterproductive. When *Investigations* is used as the context for reading and study-skills courses, then the students can practice new strategies using the content of the workbook (see Appendix D). When it's used as a credit-bearing course, then, as noted, the expectation is that the facilitator brings to the classroom relevant readings and other materials to deepen or broaden the scope.
- ***"Is this actually working?"*** The first time you work with the material you'll likely wonder if it's working. Resist the urge to react to all the things that worry you. After you've gone through the workbook a couple of times, you should be better able to trust the process and know that many concerns resolve themselves as part of the process itself.

A Request

We ask that the first time you use the workbook you follow the process and observe the results before considering modifications. Our experience with the original workbook *Getting Ahead in a Just-Gettin'-By World,* which already has been used in a number of community settings, suggests that the best results come from adhering closely to the philosophy and sequence you'll find here. As you become familiar with this work, you will undoubtedly bring to it your own style and additional content and resources, but please allow yourself the time to become familiar with it as presented here. Thank you.

II. Co-Investigation as a Process of Teaching and Learning

Investigations into Economic Class in America is a transactional process, a co-investigation—with facilitator and learner continually engaged in negotiating priorities, methods, and criteria of evaluation. Adult learners want to be more independent and self-directed, yet they need to be guided toward information to build knowledge and skills. In this process students work independently and in groups to investigate issues of personal interest and relevance. The facilitator acts as co-investigator, resource, and guide.

Sequence and Reinforcement

The sequenced modules and assignments are expressly designed to build metacognitive function—to teach students how to think about their thinking and move beyond using only concrete, sensory, and story-based thinking patterns. It's important to follow the particular sequence and to reinforce the learning as you move along. Karen Becker, Karla Krodel, and Bethanie Tucker (2009) paraphrase William Coles (1992) when they say, "Assignments require students to access prior knowledge, read more about it, think more about it, and attach new ideas to what they once knew" (p. 141). Continues Coles:

> **[A]s a pedagogy, sequencing can be thought of as both a model and an argument for the value of sustained thinking:** [Q]uestions result in responses, which in turn can become the basis for more searching questions and richer, more complicated responses. In practice, then, a sequentially constructed [investigation] becomes a way for [an instructor] to offer [the investigation] to students as a mode of learning, a special way of thinking and coming to know, thereby enabling them to understand the work [of the investigation] as an activity that can have meaning, to them as students and to them as more than that. (p. 1)

Sequences support the concept of "rolling revisions" of earlier work. Students revisit information (as well as the journals and writing assignments if they are used) and revise based on new information or new understanding of earlier concepts. Knowledge is reinforced as new layers are added. See Appendixes A and B for condensed descriptions of the purpose of each module and the embedded sequences.

Moving from Situated Cognition to a Culture of Learning

The workbook begins by "meeting the students where they are" and honoring the knowledge about poverty they bring to the classroom. As first articulated by Karla Krodel, Karen Becker, Henry Ingle, and Susan Jakes (2008), "Situated learning occurs in a context (in this case, the context of economic class) within a set of relationships and social norms" (p. 7)—the group process that develops in the classroom. At the outset, the purpose is not to learn *from* talk but to learn *to* talk as the key to participation (Lave & Wenger, 1991). The facilitator works collaboratively to review, edit, and apply quality-assurance approaches to students' work through learning opportunities that draw on James Surowiecki's (2005) "wisdom of learning from the crowds" theory. The process creates learner-generated content "not prescribed by teachers acting as dispensers of information but rather content discovered and created *by the students* [emphasis added] as they become actively engaged in the construction of the knowledge base they perceive to be needed in their real world" (pp. 7–8). Krodel et al. go on to say that:

> This participation creates a shared repertoire of vocabulary, communal routines, and behaviors (Wenger, 1999) and fosters the relationships and extra support needed to move to formalized or decontextualized education (p. 7) ... **Indeed, this approach to learning prepares students for their new roles in school and society by using life itself as the context for education rather than positioning education as the preparation necessary for life.** (p. 8)

The following chart outlines how the major elements of *Investigations* interact to effect this change.

Changing Thinking from Situated Cognition to a Culture of Learning

Using *Investigations into Economic Class in America*

	Beginning stages of *Investigations* 'Just plain folks'	Intermediate and ending phase of *Investigations* Student	Ending phase and post-*Investigations* Practitioner
Reasons with	**Causal stories** Students examine personal stories as the context for the course	**Laws** Students apply hidden rules of economic class to understand their past and present societal experience	**Causal models** Students use the poverty Research Continuum and process of change as analytical frameworks to support abstract arguments
Acting on	**Situations** Students act on current situations, building *bonding* relationships and peer support within the group	**Symbols** Students create mental models reflecting personal and community resources, building *bridging* relationships; students increase their support for each other	**Conceptual situations** Increasingly complicated mental models represent social, political, and economic issues to address

	Beginning stages of *Investigations* 'Just plain folks'	Intermediate and ending phase of *Investigations* Student	Ending phase and post-*Investigations* Practitioner
Resolving	**Emergent problems and dilemmas** Students apply new learning and accept support from new relationships	**Well-defined problems** Students proactively plan and collaborate to meet goals and build resources identified in personal resource assessment	**Ill-defined problems** Students engage in and seek new relationships to support plans and solve problems identified in personal and community resource assessment; they predict problems and are proactive in approaching new situations
Producing	**Negotiable meaning and socially constructed understanding** Students build community and shared language to understand economic class	**Fixed meaning and immutable concepts** Students establish a lexicon and framework of ideas that can be applied to individual plans	**Negotiable meaning and socially constructed understanding** Students use new language to reflect on issues, assign meaning, and build new relationships to support change

Note. Adapted from "Situated Cognition and the Culture of Learning," by J. S. Brown, A. Collins, and P. Duguid, 1989, *Educational Researcher, 18*(1), p. 35. Copyright 1989 by American Educational Research Association.

Co-Investigation

Through co-investigation and discussions, students use *critical-thinking skills* to get more information, to analyze, and to evaluate topics—such as the impact of public policy on communities and individuals' economic status, what constitutes a living wage, and how economic class has affected the availability of resources in one's personal life. The assessments and planning processes develop *practical thinking skills* that help students learn to answer questions, solve problems (proactively), and make decisions. The co-investigative process in *Investigations* teaches students "how to be students" in other academic settings as well, also developing higher level skills for practical action beyond the campus.

The sequenced co-investigation (1) builds on prior knowledge and (2) puts the students in charge of developing the content. This is the foundation for teaching and learning. What follows is a description of several strategies and approaches that work well in this context.

Mental Models

These are used throughout this workbook to define what is known and how the knowledge changes. Michael Fairbanks (2000, pp. 271–272) identifies four principles for mental models:

1. A mental model consists of beliefs, inferences, and goals that are first-person, concrete, and specific. It is a mental map of how the world works.

2. Mental models are sets of beliefs that are pro-innovative or anti-innovative.
3. Mental models shape performance and can be tested against objectives.
4. Mental models can be changed.

Peter Senge (1990) describes mental models as theories-in-use; some are simple generalizations, and some are complicated, but they determine how we act: "The problems with mental models lie not in whether they are right or wrong—by definition, all models are simplifications. The problems with mental models arise when the models are tacit—when they exist below the level of awareness" (p. 176). **If you are not aware of your mental models, you cannot challenge them, and so they become a barrier to learning. They keep you frozen where you are.**

Investigations uses intentional mental models to accelerate learning and help students:

1. Make fast and large jumps between concrete observations of things (behaviors, situations, people, environments, relationships, activities) and abstract generalizations (analyses, labels).
2. Say what is not normally said; articulate the tacit knowledge behind the observations and generalizations.
3. Investigate honestly by balancing inquiry and advocacy.
4. Expose the differences between what we say (espoused theories) and what we do (theories-in-use) (Senge, 1990, p. 186).

For our purposes, mental models can be drawings, stories, analogies cartoons, or physical movements that assist memory and accelerate learning. They are especially helpful in collapsing large amounts of information and expressing a larger, abstract concept. For example, they can be used to represent concepts and their component parts (such as poverty in Module 2) or processes (such as the process of change in Module 3 and stages of change in Module 8). Below is a mental model for the European Reformation.

Mental Model for European Reformation

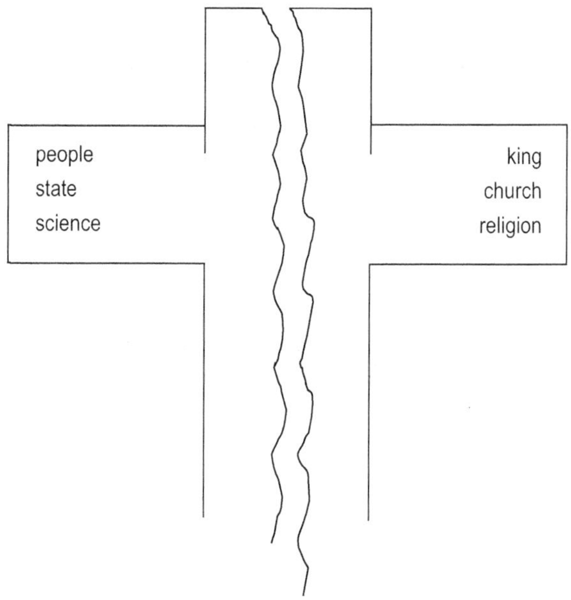

Note. From *Mental Models for Social Studies/History: Grades 6–12* (p. 125), 2008, Highlands, TX: aha! Process. Adapted with permission.

A series of personal and group mental models will be generated, as concepts about economic class are explored. *They should be created in such a way that the group can retrieve and revise them at will.* Low-tech methods, such as flipchart paper, work fine. The point is that the mental models provide the means to conceptualize the information generated by the investigation, and they need to be accessible during each class period so students can build upon them, revise them, and discover connections among them.

Language

According to Kenneth Dowst (1980), "[T]he way we use language ... seems not only to reflect but in part to determine what we know, what we can do, and in a sense, who we are" (p. 72). Language modifies the self and creates reality. Gaps in language skills can be bridged more quickly through the desire to communicate and excitement generated by the subject matter in *Investigations.*

Module 6 focuses specifically on issues of language use—including language acquisition, discourse and story patterns, voice, conflict resolution/negotiation, and code switching—as they relate to the casual and formal registers of English. All the modules, however, offer opportunities to accelerate language development, building a resource key to learning, imagination, and communication.

Building Vocabulary

Each module adds new words to the "Lexicon"—an intentionally formal title that draws attention to a word list of terms and concepts the group uses to describe various aspects of economic class and the process of change. Adding to the lexicon, which is under development by the students, becomes a tool for fostering *word consciousness* and promoting *shared meaning* and understanding. You can foster word consciousness through modeling interest and curiosity about new words, recognizing and encouraging the use of new words, using correct pronunciation, and playing with words (including appropriate humor). As the sequence unfolds, the words are used many times in many contexts. Encourage students to use their new language skills first to build understanding of their individual stories, then to reflect on issues and assign meaning to external events—a higher level of cognition. Web-based tools, such as *www.dictionary.com,* are helpful resources.

Select words from the lexicon to model other vocabulary-building strategies. For example:

Sketching

Remind students that their mental models are sometimes also definitions. Consider the mental models of Story Structure and Discourse Patterns (Module 6). Have students develop illustrations for the lexicon of this course.

Semantic Maps

Semantic maps might help students build vocabulary, capture elements of the concepts, and improve their ability to express complex ideas. Semantic maps help students learn the key components of a definition by answering three questions (Becker et al., 2009, p. 113):

- What is it?
- What is it like?
- What are some examples?

It is more useful to work this material out with students on chart paper or via a computer projector—or assign it as an investigation—than provide it to students through lecture. Examples of semantic mapping from Module 6's lexicon appear in Appendix D. Classroom technologies, such as Smart boards and computer projectors that allow students to see/read what the facilitator is creating, also may be useful.

Wide Reading

This describes the sort of extensive reading on a given topic that results in multiple exposures to new vocabulary. Research shows that students learn a portion of new definitions from the context and that repeated exposure reinforces learning. Listen to identify topics covered in this course that are interesting to each student—and individually encourage students to read more about their interest areas. Such acts of recognition also promote a positive relational learning environment. If students have trouble understanding what they read, sit down one on one and help them find answers within the text to their questions, such as these:

- What is the main idea of the passage?
- Why did the author write this passage? What does the author give you reason to believe?
- Why is this information important to the reader?
- How does the author make his or her point clear? (e.g., examples, lists, comparisons, etc.)
- How does the author expect the reader to react to the passage? (note basic information, change an opinion, move to action, etc.)
- What conclusions can be drawn from this passage?
- What are the opinions vs. facts in the passage?
- If the author had been _______, how might the passage have been different?

Note. Adapted from *Understanding and Engaging Under-Resourced College Students* (pp. 136–137), by K. A. Becker, K. M. Krodel, and B. H. Tucker, 2009, Highlands, TX: aha! Process. Copyright 2009 by aha! Process.

Encourage students to read more about their diverse interests and to analyze what they read using the lens of economic class—for example, the class hierarchy of musical instruments and musical style, with jazz guitar being at one end and classical piano at the other, or literature describing the stories of various groups of individuals from different classes. Be concrete in your support of additional reading. Show short excerpts of movies based on books that deal with class, and put books on reserve in the library. We have provided lists of additional material related to the content of the modules, as well as films, literature, and poetry related to economic class. Updated lists are available at *www.gettingaheadnetwork.com/college* where we welcome additions (yours and those of your students) to this community of practice.

Reading Effectively

Depending again on what types of additional readings are used, you also have the opportunity to teach reading skills directly, such as how to:

- Skim or survey material to get an overview
- Read chunks of material thoroughly to discover patterns and make notes about the content
- Compare two different sources of information on the same topic

Many campuses have centers or programs to help students strengthen their reading skills. Pairing *Investigations* with a dedicated reading course, if this is available on your campus, is another way to increase student exposure to diverse content, build reading and language skills, and help students see the relevance of and connections among their courses.

Writing Assignments

The journal assignments and writing assignments are offered with the assumption that you (the facilitator) are not a writing instructor. As in the case of using additional readings, you will determine how much or little emphasis to put on journaling and whether to use the additional writing assignments. At one end of the spectrum, the journals can be simple reactions to or reflections on the information and the *Investigations* material. In that case, the journal entries serve to document the process under way. If you review student journals, you are able to continually assess the group's progress and monitor for any unusual issues. At the other end of the spectrum, writing assignments can be used to develop college-level writing skills and additional knowledge about the content.

There is additional information about working with student writing assignments in "Responding to Student Writing" (Appendix C). This appendix—as well as the information about code switching in Module 6 and the *Facilitator Notes* for Module 6—advocate for concentrating on students' thinking and ability to express and develop ideas rather than marking grammar, spelling, punctuation, and other mechanical elements.

Questioning Techniques

The discussion questions in the workbook are designed to help process and develop the information presented in the workbook and by the students. The questions are usually worded in such a way as to *separate the problem from the person* and avoid "leading" answers. You might begin a discussion by asking a student to choose a question and respond to it. Encourage other students to add to the response—or you might pick up on other questions and instigate discussion. It isn't necessary to ask and answer every question.

Encourage students to sharpen their thinking, use more precise language, and make the connections between ideas or between content and process. In the workbook this is called "tight thinking," and you can encourage it through recognition and feedback.

Root Causes Through 'The 5 Whys'

"The 5 Whys" is a strategy to reveal root causes of problems and issues—and can help students get past superficial responses in the classroom, in their writing assignments, and in brainstorming sessions. (Note that this isn't a constructive negotiation technique, as "why" questions are often perceived as aggressive.)

In this example, Lee Jenkins (2004) gets to the root cause of a problem: The base of one particular monument is beginning to disintegrate, while another nearby is sound.

- ***Why? The other monument has the same base, and it is fine.*** Because it gets hosed down every day.
- ***Why?*** Because there too many bird droppings on it.
- ***Why are there more bird droppings here?*** The birds are attracted because there are so many spiders to eat.
- ***Why are there more spiders (and hence birds) at this monument than the other?*** Because there are more flying insects for the spiders to eat.
- ***Why are there more flying insects?*** Because they turn the lights on at this monument an hour earlier than the other.

Such a series of questions might reveal simple and effective answers (turn the lights on later rather than replacing the base of the monument).

Technology

Tools ranging from social media to virtual classroom technologies offer possibilities for developing knowledge and relationships, as well as maintaining a high level of interactive contact with students. Unfortunately, the "digital divide" is a reality that leaves many under-resourced students feeling even more behind the curve on campus. If this gap in both skill and access to computer resources is accounted for, perhaps by pairing *Investigations* with a computer literacy course, then these new media tools may prove beneficial. Another option might be to choose only one or two applications that will likely also be used in other courses.

Most campuses offer computer labs for student use. However, mere access is insufficient. If the need for tech support is not intentionally planned for and addressed, you can expect to find yourself filling that role and spending valuable class hours teaching technology skills. If you don't take the "tech gap" into account, more students probably will drop out.

III. The Role of Facilitation in the Process of Teaching and Learning

Listening is an attitude (Farson, 1997). Listening precedes dialog; dialog precedes action (Senge, 1990).

Your role as facilitator is to assist the process of self-discovery in such a way that *students recognize and articulate their own motivation for change*—if in fact they choose to make changes in their lives. You will guide the group's process, point to sources of information, and support the development of independent and informed ideas and conclusions.

If you recognize the fundamental difference between the model presented in this workbook—the instructor as facilitator and co-investigator, "the guy on the side," as opposed to "the sage on the stage," which is the instructor role in more traditional college classes—then it will be clear that you must set the tone early by listening, by reversing the flow of information. Listening bridges distrust and builds relationships. If you are to listen and facilitate the discussion, then you cannot provide or prescribe conclusions or solutions. "Accurate empathy, non-possessive warmth, and genuineness" (Miller & Rollnick, 2002, p. 6) create a student-centered relationship. A sense of humor, the willingness to relax professional boundaries a bit, and have some fun along the way help greatly in establishing the collaborative atmosphere.

Build Knowledge of the Content Areas

It's important to develop your own knowledge base about economic class and the causes and effects of poverty. This would include ongoing investigation of the ethnic, racial, and religious characteristics of the participating students, as well as the pertinent political and economic circumstances affecting the surrounding community and the nation as a whole. If you have your own investigations under way, you become an authentic co-investigator and learner alongside the students. Students will appreciate your genuine curiosity and willingness to explore with them.

Don't underestimate what you can learn from your students. A curious and nonjudgmental attitude is essential both in facilitating someone else's self-discovery and in learning from students about their lives. One of the premises here is that acquiring bridging social capital—relationships with people from other classes, cultures, and backgrounds—is necessary for under-resourced students to further their plans for a more stable life. Likewise, you, as a *de facto* member of the dominant (middle- or upper-class) culture, are encouraged to seek out and build mutually respectful relationships with people from poverty. Such relationships provide an authentic and ongoing source of knowledge that enables you to validate or correct perceptions and interpretations of behaviors and situations.

Maintain Two Story Lines

You will be working with two story lines throughout this workbook. One story is the collective narrative of *all* people in poverty, including the impact of poverty on the larger community and society. The second story line is about the personal impact of poverty on individuals: their history and the degree to which they have specific resources.

The role of the facilitator is to separate poverty from the person. When you ask, "How has poverty affected you?" you help create *intellectual distance or detachment* that facilitates abstract thinking and integration of information. When you fail to separate the problem (poverty) from the person you seem to blame the individual for his or her circumstances without regard to local or national issues. Separating the two means the student can develop more objective opinions and arguments rather than defending his or her honor.

Build Relationships of Mutual Respect

Work to intentionally establish a cooperative, relational learning environment. Given that relationships are a driving force for students from poverty, you're encouraged to be especially intentional about how and why you relate to students. There are those who resist being "friends" with students and those who actively seek to nurture and support. Relational learning does not mean one has to inquire about students' offspring, spouse, parents, or pets—nor does it mean one must provide services outside of class above and beyond what the syllabus promises. But relational learning also doesn't preclude such actions. What is most important is to be authentic, empathetic, respectful, and enthusiastic vis-à-vis students' knowledge and learning—without "normalizing" your own experience at the expense of theirs (see Choice, Power, and Accountability on the next page). Following are some practical methods to achieve that sense of *support, insistence, high expectations, and accountability.* Sources are Clark Moustakas (1966), Stephen Brookfield (1990), Robert Marzano (2007), and Ruby Payne (2005, 2008).

Support

When directly teaching content, process, and mental models:

- Foster a sense of mutual respect through the co-investigative process
- Create a positive, constructive peer group to belong to by collaboratively establishing group rules for an emotionally and physically safe class environment
- Be explicit about how the course is organized; about the purpose of class activities, projects, and readings; and about the process at work
- Objectively present information for investigation; don't defend it or take a "side"
- Show concern; listen carefully to students and reinforce what motivates them
- Discover and acknowledge—in class or out of class—at least one interest, passion, skill, or talent for each student, especially if it relates to the content of the course

- Avoid showing favoritism toward an individual or subgroup of the class or indicating bias against students who don't perform well
- Be aware that intent and attitudes drive body language, and many students are skilled at reading nonverbal communication

Insistence

Regarding the motivation and persistence that come from the relationship:

- Be consistent in what you say and do—or students will have reason not to trust you
- Do what you say you will do; avoid breaking promises
- Coach and advocate; provide positive bridging social capital within your personal boundaries
- Share aspects of yourself appropriately; explain what drew you to this workbook or how you became passionate about teaching
- Provide students access to previously under-resourced individuals who attained success, yet maintained connectedness to their roots
- Hold the students accountable to themselves, to you, and to the group

High Expectations

"I know you can and you will, even when you don't think you can" is demonstrated by providing adult-oriented, college-level work rather than lowering expectations. For example:

- Have high expectations of yourself as well and avoid undermining your own credibility in an effort to affirm the student
- Cooperate by being open to change that is congruent with your vision for the course
- Be cognizant of your influence as a role model
- Connect aspects of the course and its content to students' individual interests, passions, skills, and talents
- Don't "lower the bar"; enforce expectations consistently—and be clear if/when certain expectations are being waived and why that is happening

Choice, Power, and Accountability

Accountability is a positive attribute when it arises from within the person as a result of his or her use of choice and power. This form of accountability is productive. Productive accountability has these characteristics:

- People are accountable to themselves and others—and especially to the group itself
- Expectations are communicated clearly, concretely, and respectfully; information is presented in a way that is relevant, including information about accountability
- The expectations for participation and assignments are related to the systems and structures of the classroom and the school
- Accountability is framed as choices with natural and logical consequences
- If consequences are applied, they are handled face to face, not by letter, phone, or e-mail; in this way mediation can occur, and the relationship can be maintained

When facilitating *Investigations,* recognize that the material also is relevant to you. Monitor yourself for hidden or subconscious agenda, biases, stereotypes, and rules. As the students create mental models of life in poverty, middle class, and wealth, develop a model for your own economic and societal experience. If you were raised in a stable middle-class environment, be careful that you don't assume that what was "normal" for you will be normal for everyone else. Each individual has his or her own worldview or mindset. Rushing to judgment is often an indication that a person has normalized his or her own experience. Learn the hidden rules of poverty in Module 5 and evaluate your accountability measures in light of them. How might your approach to accountability be modified to avoid a punitive connotation (yet maintain high expectations)? For example …

When low-income students come to college the expectation is that they come to class on time and complete their assignments. This is made explicit through group discussions and the use of concrete examples and written communications. When the student doesn't meet the expectations, the conversation about accountability is conducted face to face: "What happened? What other choices could you have made? What could you do next time? Let's make a plan. What choices do you need to make?" The consequences are explained. The next time the expectations aren't met, the consequences take place but with a conversation, for example: "You are being dropped as a result of your choice not to meet the attendance requirement." All the steps above are part of a respectful process.

Giving Feedback

M. A. Horstman (n.d.) advocates using all three of the following methods for obtaining and providing feedback:

- One-on-one meetings between just you and the student should occur at least at the midpoint and end of the term—and almost any time the student requests a meeting; these meetings might be about performance or to clarify understanding of content
- Feedback: The purpose of feedback is to improve future behavior; feedback statements follow a clearly delineated format:

  (Ask) "May I give you some feedback?"

  (Describe the behavior) "When you do A *(describe the impact)* then B (C, D) happens"

  (Discuss future behavior)

    (Approving) "That is great; keep it up"

    or

    (Correcting) "What do you think you can do differently next time?"
- Coaching is more goal-oriented and long-term; set short-term goals (usually 1–2 weeks) that are milestones along a long-term goal track; this is particularly used in the backwards planning processes incorporated throughout; under-resourced students generally need a lot of support and coaching to learn how to use planning skills to their benefit

Voices

Model the adult voice (as opposed to the parent or child voice, as described in Module 6). The ability to translate between the formal and casual registers is helpful, but use your own authentic voice—and be cautious about using the casual register if it isn't natural for you.

The Paradox Among Roles

Instructor or Facilitator?

In the original *Getting Ahead* model, the facilitator has no particular power, control over, or responsibility for the investigators. The relationship there is far more that of co-equals. If this workbook is used as a credit-bearing course, then you must serve as facilitator/co-investigator *and* arbiter of a grade. If *Investigations* is used for graded credit or to demonstrate a performance benchmark or level of achievement, then there is an automatic shift in power toward the facilitator/instructor. Below are suggestions for addressing this imbalance.

- Describe your own investigations: What are you learning? Facilitators tend to be better accepted by the group if they also are doing their own investigations.
- Be explicit about when you are entering "instructor mode" defined by assigning or returning graded reading, writing, presentation, or homework assignments. Make liberal use of one-on-one conferences to discuss performance, metrics, and outcomes.
- Use the co-facilitator model whereby one person facilitates the discussions and investigations, while the other makes and grades assignments.
- Examine grading options; is it possible to grade a simple pass/fail or credit/no credit?

As these ideas increasingly are applied in higher education settings, we welcome the addition of your experience and solutions to this conundrum.

Facilitator Role as Someone from the Dominant Culture

Defining a Dominated Group

According to the perspectives of people in the dominant group, members of a dominated group share a common fate, and it's usually not good. Individuals from a distinct racial, ethnic, or religious group, such as recent immigrants from Cambodia or Africa, are likely to identify themselves with the group and recognize that their fate is linked with the others. People from poverty could be considered a dominated group in America. However, some people in poverty feel part of the dominant culture—as with poor whites, for example, and working-class people who work multiple jobs and still can't meet basic needs. Some students may for the first time begin to identify themselves as being in poverty and part of a dominated group.

As facilitator, be aware that this dynamic may be occurring, but try not to assign students to categories. Failure to recognize and account for your position representing the dominant culture can interfere with your credibility. There are several activities in the *Facilitator Notes* to help you address power disparities by explicitly examining race, normalization, and the experience of racism (see below).

Systemic Racism

Racism is a background constant in North American society. The following brief commentary on "The Four Features of Racism" (Becker et al., 2009, p. 11, based on Valenzuela & Addington, 2006a) describes some of the contours of this constant. The Four Features of Racism can validate the experience and intuition of people of color and shift the perspectives of whites so that they become intentionally aware of the daily advantages and disadvantages precipitated by racial identity.

1. **Race matters.** Compared with many countries in the world, the history of the United States is short. Though laws have been passed to change racial, political, economic, and social injustices (including segregation), racial identity still makes a difference, still "invoking mythological moral and intellectual superiority and inferiority."
2. **Racism is more than the historical black-white dichotomy.** This country's early laws and policies required definition of white and nonwhite. In the past, nonwhite primarily meant black. Today the black/white dichotomy affects every community of color by paradoxically resulting in blindness to the issues of such other communities as Native Americans.
3. **Racism and other oppressions intersect.** Race, gender, and economic class are so interrelated that some would argue one can't address one without accounting for the other two. Like economic class, "race shapes how we experience other socially defined identities." Race, gender, and class are relative to each other. "A white man's experience of gender is dramatically different [from] a black man's. Race is the most powerful factor … in how one experiences other systemic oppressions."
4. **Identity formation, or racialization, is the core feature of racism that reveals its forcefulness.** In the United States, we're all assigned, for life, to a racial category that also holds social meaning. Even the national census every decade underscores the importance of identifying oneself by race. Racialization shapes individual, institutional, and cultural identity with cumulative and synergistic effects. Racism is enacted every day upon individuals—and broadly within communities and political and economic structures.

Perception Is Reality

Whether you are from the middle class—or once were (or still are) in poverty and are now working in the middle-class world of higher education (and there are many)—you will most likely be *perceived* by the students as being from the dominant culture and hence will need to consciously work to build trust and mutually respectful relationships. Those who have worked on poverty or diversity issues are familiar with the quandary of the facilitator's hierarchical position. There is no escaping two conflicting yet co-existing realities. One is the distrust that many people in poverty have for authority and institutions. This can be ameliorated, but only somewhat, if the facilitator is from poverty, because he or she is an employee of the school and/or may be a member of some other group that disqualifies him or her from automatic credibility. The second reality is that facilitators have something positive to offer investigators.

Raising the Difficult Issues

As a representative of the dominant culture, be prepared to be the one to raise the issues that usually affect people in the dominated group—inadequate housing, low-wage jobs, predators, racism, unfair banking practices, and so on. When those who are dominated raise these issues, it *puts them into the role of complainer or radical*—and may even suggest that they are speaking for the dominated group. Being forced into one of those roles detracts from the development of new roles as mediator, creative thinker, or leader (Lobovits & Prowell, 1996, pp. 3–5). When the *facilitator* raises a controversial issue, however, the people from the dominated group tend to be freer to respond.

The Facilitation of Group Process

The interactive nature of *Investigations* fosters the evolution of group process. People in groups tend to act in predictable ways. Bruce Tuckman (1965) describes the stages of group development as forming, storming, norming, and performing. Each stage contains activities that the group must go through in order to achieve the next level of development. His theory is that a new group must go through all these stages in order to reach the final stage of performing. Some ideas for supporting group development in relation to the *Investigations* process are described below.

Forming

In this phase the students are just getting together and are still more a collection of individuals than a team or a group. Students get to know each other, set up routines (when we meet, where, simple things). There is a deliberate avoidance of conflict, and group members are guarded and hesitant—mostly watching and gaining an understanding of each other and the group.

Setting the stage: In the beginning, your goal as facilitator is to establish a comfortable "around the kitchen table" atmosphere that encourages conversation. The process undertaken in this workbook does not resemble the typical classroom environment. There is no lecturing, no PowerPoint presentation, and no one standing at the head of the class. Therefore, take great pains to configure classroom seating so that students are around an actual table (tables pushed together) or sitting on chairs in a circle; you are part of that circle. Traditional row seating has a negative impact on the group process.

Specific activities and actions:

- Have the group establish ground rules that set boundaries and promote respect and safety (suggestions to build upon appear in Module 1)
- Start each session by getting agreement as to the agenda for the day; use the learning objectives table at the start of each module to describe *what* will be covered, *why* it's important, and *how* it's personally relevant
- Establish patterns and rituals; start each session with questions or activities that get everyone talking and established as a member of the group that day—for example: *Naming/Listing Problems;* as students arrive there may be casual conversation about concrete problems that derail educational plans (sick children, crime, job loss, illness, etc.); have a student volunteer start an ongoing list of these barriers to everyday life—and to getting out of poverty; identifying this information as important is affirming to the students who are reporting the problems

Once the process of change has been introduced in Module 3, the items on the list can be described as "concrete." You can keep the group moving by explaining that the more time spent talking about being stuck in the concrete, the less time there is to talk about getting ahead. Do this with respect and awareness in order to avoid the sense that you have "shut down" the student.

When you start doing mental models, invite (but do not require) people to share their models. The idea is to use one another's thinking to build clearer, more specific models. A classroom with dedicated space to store mental models is helpful; the models should be visible for easy reference all semester.

Finally, don't forget that even the quieter group members are probably learning. If someone just doesn't want to verbalize, allow him or her to "pass." But occasionally give opportunities for the less verbal students also to have a turn to speak.

Storming

In this phase, the group is serious about accomplishing the goals, and members likely will have differing opinions and objectives. These will lead to conflict for some; others will withdraw (a conflict resolution technique). During this stage the roles and responsibilities of group members will start to be defined as students push their ideas or compete for leadership.

Overcoming resistance: There may be a resistance to the information about economic class. Resistance comes from students if they feel stereotyped, labeled, or judged. Emphasize that this work is based on patterns—and there are many exceptions to these patterns. Stay focused on economic realities and show that *these patterns arise out of economic environments and not the other way around.* It isn't your job to defend the material in the workbook or to persuade the investigators to accept it. Your role is to help the students *investigate* the information. If you encounter resistance to the ideas, cover them generally and ask students to observe people and situations around them for a few days to see if they can find examples that illustrate the material.

The paradigm shift from typical high school education to this self-directed form of learning through investigation may be another source of resistance. There may be demands to be "taught" and resistance to the need to "investigate." Capitalize on this phase of the group process to create certain healthy tensions essential to learning. Parker Palmer (1998) describes six paradoxical tensions to build into the teaching and learning space; these are highly congruent with the *Investigations* process:

1. The space should be bounded and open.
2. The space should be hospitable and "charged."
3. The space should invite the voice of the individual and the voice of the group.
4. The space should honor the "little" stories of the students and the "big" stories of the disciplines and tradition.
5. The space should support solitude and be surrounded with the resources of the community.
6. The space should welcome both silence and speech. (p. 74)

As the facilitator, you may want to return to the ground rules established in Modules 1 and 2 and incorporate all or some of Palmer's statements above. Doing so makes your expectations explicit and provides a means of describing some of the future conversations that will occur. If you find yourself getting defensive, hear yourself "preaching," or sense that you're getting angry or judgmental, you're allowing your emotions to have too much influence, which will be counterproductive for the group as well. Take a break and identify the value that you hold dear that was being challenged, then work to achieve intellectual detachment with regard to the issue.

This is also the time when some students stop coming to class. This is a painful process for some, and they may also stop coming as a way of distancing themselves from the pain. Consider ways to follow up with students to support their persistence.

Specific activities and actions:

Establish additional patterns and rituals or replace old ones. For example, do a "round robin" at the beginning of each session, asking each person to answer a question. Examples might be:

- "What is one thing you remember from the last session?"
- "Give one example of something we talked about (a cause of poverty, a hidden rule, the use of a language register) that you observed since the last meeting"

In some instances it can be beneficial to announce the round-robin topic prior to the time of the meeting. It's a good idea to establish a time limit on the answers in order to give everyone a chance to say something.

Norming

In this phase the conflict begins to subside as the group has set down rules of behavior and procedure. The rules are both written and unwritten. Because of the storming phase, students have a better understanding of each other and often develop a respectful disagreement or discourse. It is at this point that the group frequently achieves its first minor success as a group. There is still some conflict, and activities are often uncoordinated. Two members may work on the same task, or a task may be neglected because each member thought someone else was doing it. As the group becomes settled and more efficient, greater amounts of material can be covered more quickly.

Specific activities and actions:

- Break the group into sets of two or three people and have them discuss a point or do an activity, then report back to the larger group (for example, the Module 5 investigation into hidden rules could be divided among the students in the class)
- Use some of the activities as in-class group projects or take-home group projects (be aware that daily demands of work, home, and school can make group work outside of class time prohibitive)
- Establish additional patterns and rituals or replace old ones with those that allow recognition and self-disclosure

Performing

At this stage, the group is "in the zone." Groups that achieve the performing stage have high levels of trust and interdependency. Group members can focus on their work knowing that other members are doing their part as well. Students often know each other's strengths and weaknesses, then adapt group behavior around these. The students are at ease with each other and often have become friends. The group can develop a unique identity, complete with inside jokes and communication shorthand.

Students in performing groups are working hard, building on each other's ideas. Watch for interpersonal support among the students and encourage the development of their network to keep supporting each other after the end of the course. Consider one or more "after groups." How might the group—and its spirit of camaraderie and support—be sustained after the semester ends?

Other Duties as Assigned

Student Co-Facilitators

Investigations can be co-facilitated by a previous student participant who has some training in group leadership. Training and paying a student co-facilitator assigns greater value to the process and provides evidence of the school's belief that students themselves can be change leaders. The joint effort of a faculty member with a student co-facilitator has many benefits—both real and symbolic—to all involved. Student co-facilitators:

- Make the material more relevant
- Help bridge initial distrust or skepticism by students
- Build institutional capacity through the creation of experts within the student body
- Create bridging social capital
- Inform the facilitator's performance
- Earn experience and respect by assisting you
- Model healthy behavior and investigation skills
- Assist in the translation from formal to casual and casual to formal
- Can follow up personally with students who miss class

Note. Adapted from *Facilitator Notes for Getting Ahead in a Just-Gettin'-By World* (p. 12), by P. E. DeVol, 2006, Highlands, TX, aha! Process. Copyright 2006 by aha! Process.

The role of student co-facilitators should be made clear to investigators. Investigators might benefit from occasional reminders that the student co-facilitator plays no role in the grading process.

Managing Personal Problems

As the investigators uncover new information and consider aspects of their lives differently, they frequently expose or re-expose personal issues running the gamut of human experience. At times, the tension between what is now and what could be feels almost unbearable—or the pressures and stressors of today appear insurmountable. People react very differently to the material, but if a student is expressing feelings of hopelessness, has suicidal or homicidal ideation, or seems to have concrete plans to hurt self or someone else, it's time to make a referral and support that person in obtaining professional help. Take the time to investigate campus and community mental health services, and have this information readily available to students. Remember, this investigative process can in some cases become intense and trigger strong feelings on the part of students who may be facing, for the first time, certain deep and painful issues in their lives.

It is common for students to freely share the challenging, problematic circumstances of their lives and relationships, and this might feel overwhelming to new facilitators who initially feel the need to intervene, find solutions, and fix problems. **Your job, however, is to listen, question, support, and guide—not manage, tell, or solve.** The resiliency and resourcefulness you likely will observe in the students over time will help you recognize that the investigators are learning to work out their issues using new information and skills.

Managing the Time

It's important to get to the end of the workbook, to complete the process, and to come to a sense of closure. Therefore, managing the timeline for the semester or term is very important. We've offered estimates for the time needed for specific activities, but there will be a great deal of variability. At times it may feel like you are rushing through or not fully "teaching" the content. That is less a problem in this course than others; students will pick up the information or return later to retrieve it. The goal is to keep the process moving. Again, Appendixes A and B offer overviews of course content, process, and sequences—and there is a lesson planner tool in Appendix F.

Managing Closure

At about the halfway point for the group, begin to periodically remind the students how many sessions are left, and make the reminders more frequent as the class nears conclusion. This can be easily incorporated into the planning activities that require the use of a calendar. It's important to set aside time at the end for a little celebration or acknowledgment of the accomplishments of the group. As noted at the end of the "Performing" section above, it is quite common for some of the group members to want to continue to meet, in effect to ask for *"Investigations II."* The appendixes include ideas about what your school might do to provide ongoing support—and how the students might connect to community resources that can do the same.

IV. Module-by-Module Instructions

A. Overview

Students as Investigators

We have spent some time making the case that language shapes reality and perception is reality, arguing that the co-investigative process is as important as the actual content of the course, and stating that through the investigations students themselves will generate knowledge. For these reasons, **your students, the individuals who go through this experience with you, are henceforth to be referred to as *investigators.*** Investigators are active. They question, look into things, dig for facts, look for patterns, analyze the data, and find answers. Eventually they will be answerable to themselves, and it is anticipated that they will become problem solvers in the community. Trust them, and set up the conditions for their success.

Patterns in the Workbook

Recognizing the patterns in the *Investigations* workbook will help you and the investigators move through it more easily.

The Process Triangle

Module 1 introduces the Triangle, which represents how all the elements of the workbook support action. The Triangle appears at the beginning of every module thereafter. The Triangle orients you to which elements will be addressed: understanding poverty, understanding "My Life Now," critical thinking, power, responsibility, and planning. It's a mental model of the process embedded within the course, and it's used to

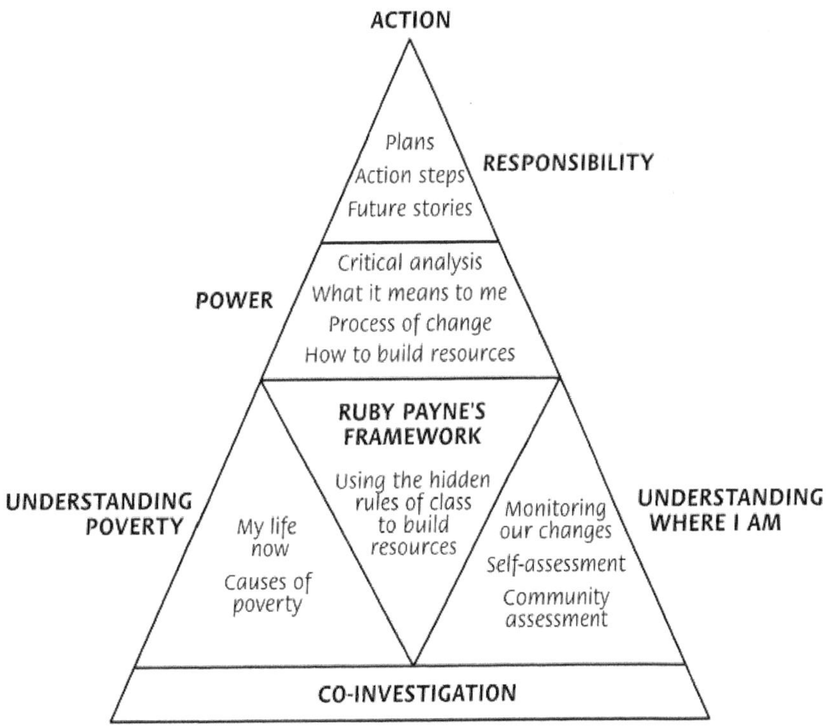

show what stage has been reached, along with the progress to date.

Learning Objectives

A "mediation" table appears at the beginning of each module. It follows the pattern of a mediated learning experience: the identification of the stimulus (the *what*), assigning meaning (the *why*), and providing a strategy (the *how*). In *Investigations* it takes the form of "what's covered" (a mini table of contents for the module), "why it's important" (the *why*), and "how it's connected to you" (how it can be used), as well as how it will be learned. Reviewing this table at the start of each class will help preview and organize the information.

The Lexicon

The lexicon contains key vocabulary appearing in the module. Encourage students to add new terms and use the vocabulary in discussions and written assignments.

Content

Each module has information about economic class and/or change theory. The following pattern organizes the elements with these headings:

> ***Information:*** Information sections (designated by Roman numerals) summarize or provide overviews of major concepts, theories, models, and ideas.
>
> ***Discussion:*** The questions to guide in-class discussion (discussions are designated by capital letters).
>
> ***Activities:*** The most important activities are the mental models that investigators are asked to create. When the workbook is complete, each student should have a series of mental models that depict his or her life and plans. Other activities take the form of worksheets, such those related to financial health metrics (activities also are designated by capital letters).

Journal Reflections

Students are asked to think about how this information relates to them personally. The act of writing further processes information and builds cognitive and language skills. A sample set of instructions for journaling appears in the appendixes.

Readings

Books and other resources relating to the module's content are annotated.

Patterns in *Facilitator Notes*

The next section of the *Facilitator Notes* provides a module-by-module overview. The elements of this overview are in the following pattern:

Concept

The overarching concepts presented in the module and the interrelationships of those concepts with the process of change are made explicit.

Sequence

This defines how the modules relate to and build upon each other.

Learning Objectives: Investigators Will ...

These sections define the knowledge, skill, and attitude changes to occur as a result of the work in the particular module.

Mental Models Labeled

This lets you see at a glance which mental models appear in each module.

Activities

Each activity presented in the module is described. NOTE: These module-by-module instructions in the *Facilitator Notes* contain optional investigations that supplement particular modules.

> ***Concept:*** As necessary, the concepts behind the activity are identified.
>
> ***Instructions:*** Additional instructions are provided as needed.
>
> ***Analysis:*** Occasionally the analysis of a given activity is made explicit.
>
> ***Sequence:*** The sequence defines how the various activities and modules interconnect and build on each other.

Writing Assignments

Examples of writing assignments that build on the information presented, support the process of individual change, and/or enhance the group process are included.

Troubleshooting and Support

The website *www.gettingaheadnetwork.com* has a tab for colleges where individuals working with this material share syllabi, activities, insights, and questions.

Congratulations!

You are about to embark upon a challenging and rewarding journey. Know that as you travel with the students you are participating in a process that has the potential to transform the life of each student. May the journey be joyful and rewarding to you as well.

MODULE 1

Getting Started

Concept

Module 1 is orientation information that can be reviewed *quickly* alongside the syllabus, but it should be reviewed *completely,* because it sets both stage and tone. If at all possible, get the group into the first activity in Module 2 during your initial meeting.

This is the students' first experience as investigators. They are the experts on their lives and communities. And this is your first opportunity to learn from them. In *Learning to Listen, Learning to Teach,* Jane Vella (2002) says, "The initial meeting between teacher and learner has to demonstrate the sense of inquiry and curiosity felt by the teacher" (p. 11).

Learning Objectives: Investigators Will ...

- Begin forming as a group
- Clarify expectations, roles, and responsibilities
- Begin the planning processes by using a calendar/date planner
- Become familiar with the workbook (and syllabus if used)

Mental Model Labeled

- Process Triangle

Activities

There are no specific investigations or activities in this module other than examining the workbook and syllabus, as well as making notes of due dates in a calendar if appropriate. The following are general suggestions for moving through this module.

Instructions

Take time to review and consider the information presented in the first section of this book—and how, specifically, you intend to establish a relational learning environment.

To get to the point of demonstrating your own sense of inquiry as a co-investigator, try to move through the review of Module 1 and have enough time to at least start Module 2 and complete a Mental Model of Poverty. Reading it aloud, or asking for volunteers to read sections aloud, is a surprisingly effective method of covering the material.

If you have the opportunity to meet with students *prior to* the course as part of the recruitment/screening process, use the individual session to begin building your relationship with each investigator, as well as to introduce the unique aspects of the *Investigations* process. If that isn't possible, you might point them out as you go through the module or summarize some of these distinctive features, which include:

- The group is run "kitchen table" style—in-class discussion is a major part of the course.
- It's about helping people develop and maintain a stable life.
- It's an investigation of personal experiences and the communities in which we live.
- Everyone in the group is an investigator.
- No one tells you what to do.
- You do a self-assessment so you can develop a plan for yourself.

Quickly explain how the mediation table (Learning Objectives) at the beginning of each chapter works in order to show what is covered in each module and how it is personally relevant.

Explain how the Triangle works to show the process. Use the term "mental model." If a syllabus is utilized, have students look to see when each module begins, and note when major assignments are due. If at all possible, provide or require that students purchase a small academic planner—and begin immediately filling in dates. Many institutions make these available free or as part of a "student handbook" that contains sundry college policies and procedures that will be investigated later in the course. Refer to the calendar or planner at the start of each class, and have each student update it with assignments, along with steps to completing assignments.

Introduce the idea of group rules or ground rules in order to establish a sense of safety, then actually create the list of rules during the first group session.

If time permits, ask for volunteers to take on certain roles—for example, someone to:

- Write down the problem list that surfaces at the beginning of each class
- Rearrange the chairs and tables, if that is necessary
- Help set up refreshments and clean up, if refreshments are provided

Start listening for themes, patterns, and key words that might be part of establishing group rituals, which can add cohesiveness to the group.

Given the reality of late registrations, some students might miss the first meeting, so be prepared to review what you covered in the first session the second time you meet.

Sequence

Return to Module 1 to reinforce the process, patterns, and expectations of the class throughout the course. As students move toward their final plans, it may be helpful to literally reread Module 1 and consider it in light of everything else they have been learning.

MODULE 2 Mental Model of Poverty

Concept

Based on the theories that (1) the learner's most significant resource is his or her own experience, (2) learning occurs best through contextualized situations, and (3) learners value experience and discovery, the sequence begins with a discussion of what is familiar—the experience of poverty in the community. Through the sharing of stories, observations, situations, problems, and dilemmas, the group collectively develops an abstract representation, or Mental Model of Poverty, of the concrete realities that poverty creates.

The ensuing analysis of the group Mental Model of Poverty creates mutual understanding around the experience of poverty and begins to build a lexicon for future use. Further investigation demonstrates that poverty is about much more than personal choices and actions—and that achieving economic stability can be exceedingly difficult, depending on community, state, and national factors. A series of investigations into objective aspects of wages, housing, living conditions, and financial security move from relatively "safe" to more challenging information. This information mitigates the self-condemnation and feelings of shame that many under-resourced investigators experience—and also primes the development of the learner's personal mental model of "My Life Now."

Investigators often have no clear understanding that life can be more stable, more fulfilling, and less toxically stressful. The personal "My Life Now" mental model conceptualizes the discrepancy between what life is like now and what life could be. This discrepancy creates the cognitive dissonance that is the foundational catalyst for change.

Sequence

Investigators will move from concrete to abstract thinking by creating and considering mental models as outside themselves. This helps investigators detach from emotionally charged situations by naming objective aspects of life and recognizing that there are common experiences and perceptions among group members. The process of "going to the abstract" and defining the abstract will be discussed in Module 3.

This sequence of investigative assignments examines personal income and expenses, linking investigators to the Research Continuum on the causes of poverty to be discussed in Module 4.

Learning Objectives: Investigators Will ...

- Examine their personal stories as the context for the course
- Begin to form relationships within the group and accept support from peers

- Begin the creation of a shared understanding of economic class theory through mental models and a shared lexicon of terms
- Examine factual information related to wages, housing, and saving

Mental Models Labeled

The creation of these mental models is a foundational piece for the entire course. Mental models help investigators tune in to the concrete realities of their lives, rethink meaning, and see a bigger picture. In this module investigators create:

- Group Mental Model of Poverty
- Personal Mental Model of the Floor Plan of My Apartment/House
- Personal Mental Model of "My Life Now"

Activities

I. A. Activity: Group Mental Model of Poverty

Concept

The first major activity, the creation of the Mental Model of Poverty, helps investigators tune in to the concrete realities of their lives and is a foundational piece for the entire course. It is the first time the learners are called upon to investigate. They will discover a unique feature of this course: that the investigators do the talking and are themselves the source of important information.

The mental model is the beginning or source of several strands of learning sequences. The sooner group members get to this activity the sooner they'll begin to see themselves in the investigator role.

Instructions

The investigators will create a Mental Model of Poverty. Have a volunteer draw a large circle. As the investigators provide the information, have the volunteer fill in the space. Ask:

- *What problems does a person in poverty have to solve?*
- *What do people worry most about?*
- *Where does a lot of the time and energy go?*

Avoid drawing conclusions for the group, i.e., don't "give them the answers." And do not add concepts that might be missing; let the work belong entirely to the group. Rather, encourage "tight thinking" by asking open-ended but guided questions, such as:

- *How so?*
- *In what way?*
- *Meaning what, exactly?*

The model usually includes financial concerns: low wages, trying to make ends meet, cyclical debt, and other frequent realities—such as time spent at agencies, family crises, housing problems, illness, transportation, safety, childcare, and abuse of various kinds (including domestic violence, drugs, and alcohol). Many stories will accompany the work of creating this mental model; those stories are important to hear.

Name the elements in the model. Label them—and add terms to the lexicon's language that accurately describe the impact of poverty on families and communities. Encourage use of these terms as more layers of knowing are developed. Such words and phrases as Concrete, Tyranny of the Moment, Reactive Problem Solvers, Relationships, Instability, and Interconnected and Interlocking Problems should be added to the mental model, around the edges of the circle. They become part of the learning sequence.

If the group brings up such analytical terms as "crisis living" or "chaos," ask them to provide concrete experiences of poverty that have led to those conclusions.

When the investigators are done adding concrete aspects of poverty to the mental model, use the discussion questions to round out the mental model's development by placing analytical terms around the edges of the circle. Once the analysis is complete, place the mental model on the wall so group members can refer to it and add items if they see fit.

Analysis: Moving from the concrete to the abstract is a theme or strategy that will be repeated throughout the sessions. The drawing on the wall is something the investigators can be objective about because it involves the whole community, not just the individual. They can detach, stand back, reflect, and think about the patterns they see and the meaning they ascribe to the patterns. This is what it means to "go to the abstract."

Analytical themes that previous groups have mentioned include:

- The arithmetic of life doesn't work very well when jobs don't pay much or you can't get full-time work, and housing takes up more than 30% of your income.
- Relationships are needed to survive in poverty. When you don't have money, family and friends fix your broken-down car, give you a place to stay, look after your kids, and give you something to eat. Relationships are a driving force. Once this is identified, add the term to the mental model.
- Once you get into the circle it's hard to get out. Resources are so low—and every problem takes so long to solve—that even getting to the low-paying job is difficult. And just as you start to work your way out, the federal policies pull the supports (that you need for your transition) out from under your feet.
- You get stuck living in the moment. Everything has to be done now.
- You don't have much power or influence.
- Many things in the circle are unstable.
- Things in the circle are interconnected.
- You have to go to several agencies in order to survive (agency time).
- You have to hustle to make it.
- Poverty is stressful: Being poor involves physical stressors—two or more jobs, manual labor, accidents, lack of sleep, loss of hearing, crowded conditions, lack or utilities, toxic waste dumps, muggers, and hunger. Being poor can involve psychological stressors like lack of control and predictability, repetitious, numbing work, taking orders, being the first to be laid off, numerous temporary jobs, worries about money and cars, and lack of stress relievers and social supports.
- Problems are concrete.
- People in poverty are problem solvers; take the opportunity to honor and affirm the problem-solving skills brought to bear most often by people in poverty. (They will

build on that foundation by adding planning skills.) In poverty, there's little time to plan and prevent. Problems need to be solved now: The electricity needs to be turned on now, the baby is sick, and it's the last day to pay the tuition bill. All of one's energy is consumed by the latest crisis. Resources for stability are scarce. These conditions develop reactive problem-solving skills, resiliency, and resourcefulness. These conditions also can overwhelm and even incapacitate, depending on the person and the circumstances.

MENTAL MODEL OF POVERTY

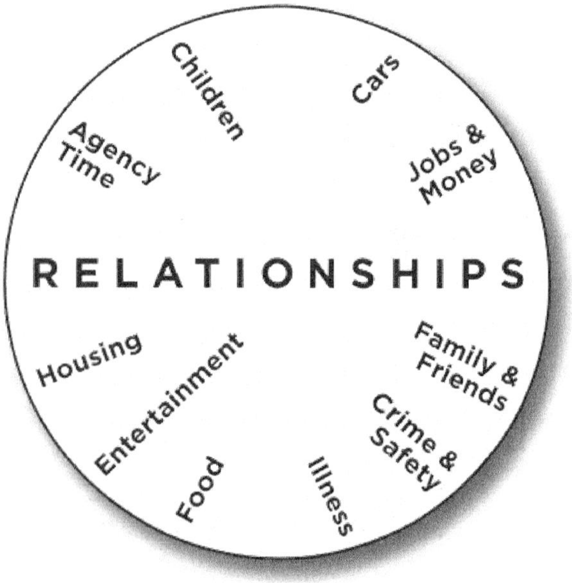

Sequence

The Mental Model of Poverty is sequenced in these ways:

- Poverty is defined as the degree to which a person does without resources; the Mental Model of Poverty tends to be a picture of low resources.
- An accurate perception of the impact poverty has on individuals and communities is necessary for planning at the personal, organizational, and community levels. This mental model can be used by all three entities to make plans; the information is specific, concrete, and local—and it can be verified. Planning takes place in Module 12.
- Income and wealth disparity is shown in Module 4. The greater the income disparity between the poor and the rich in the U.S., the more pronounced are the class distinctions. And the less power and influence people in poverty have, the harder it is for them to get out of poverty. Mental models of middle class and wealth also are found in Module 4.
- The mental models of socioeconomic class define the three environments (poverty, middle class, wealth)—out of which arise the hidden rules of class, as seen in Module 5.

II. A. Activity: The Affordable Housing Payment Threshold Calculator

Concept

The information about housing and a living wage begins to introduce the concept that poverty is about more than personal choices. Bringing abstract information to the table for the group to analyze in an investigation will reveal key features of the poverty experience. This helps investigators develop intellectual detachment from their concrete reality and consider new information as it relates to them.

Instructions

Let investigators help one another with the math. It might be helpful to break into small groups. This is usually the first place in the sequence of the *Investigations* workbook that people might express motivation for change. The "aha" moment often comes after the investigators figure out the percentage of their income that goes for housing. When they see that the arithmetic of life isn't working, some people are ready to take action immediately.

Sequence

The costs of housing activities are sequenced in these ways:

- This investigation will provide information for the "My Life Now" mental model that is done at the end of this module.
- Relates to the causes of poverty presented in Module 4.
- Creates motivation and influences the stages of change in Module 8.
- Informs the individual's self-assessment of resources in Module 9.

II. C. Activity: Mental Model of the Floor Plan of My Apartment/House

Concept

This mental model helps investigators evaluate their daily living conditions. This information is important because the students' ability to control their environment and organize their work impacts their potential success in college. This is another model to help the student examine concrete reality from an abstract perspective.

Instructions

Sketch a sample floor plan and label the rooms (kitchen, living room, bedroom, bathroom, etc.). Investigators will do the same in their journal. Ask:

- *Who is in the house in the course of a week?*
- *Who sleeps where?*
- *What makes noise, and where is it?*
- *Where do you study or keep the school books?*
- *What else happens in that space?*
- *How much privacy is there?*

Allow the group members to do this as they see fit, alone or in pairs. This mental model may need to be a private investigation. People will talk about it if they are comfortable. There is no need to press people to share with the group, but facilitators need to see what individual students came up with.

Analysis: Under-resourced investigators often live in crowded homes because the cost of housing is so high in relation to income that people double up. Lights and heat might be turned down to save on utilities. TVs and radios are usually on for entertainment and/or turned up to drown out the activities of the other people in the house. Drawing this model helps students identify physical space and times when studying is possible—or to realize the need to develop an alternate strategy. The information also begins to identify the people and relationships that surround the investigators and how these affect the concrete realities of the investigator's day.

Sequence

The Floor Plan mental model is sequenced in these ways:

- The key point in Module 5 is about giving up relationships for achievement, at least for a period of time; it establishes who is in the investigator's life.
- It may be linked to motivation and stages of change in Modules 7 and 8.
- It is linked to the Social Capital mental model in Module 7.
- It is linked to the Support for Change mental model in Module 12.

III. A. Activity: Getting Ahead or Just Getting By?

Concept

This exercise provides the connection between/among what one actually earns, what one actually pays for housing, and what one needs to earn to keep expenses reasonable for economic stability. Additional information about the minimum wage and Federal Poverty Guidelines anchors personal experience with objective data.

Instructions

Investigators are frequently confused by the Income Related to the Cost of Housing chart. It might be helpful to break into groups, then lead a slow, step-by-step oral instruction, answering the multitude of questions that might arise, including:

- *What if I never work? ... I just get a check.* (Use the amount of the monthly check.)
- *What if the amount of money I earn isn't even on the chart?* (Investigators have the affordable payment from the last exercise, so now find the current rent on the chart to determine what they need to earn in order to cover the cost of housing.)
- *What if I don't pay rent because I live with someone else?* (Use the housing payment of the person you live with.)

The ensuing discussion will anchor the investigators' story with objective information and reveal unique characteristics of the community, as well as unique personal solutions to the housing/income disparity.

Sequence

As above.

IV. A. Activity: What Is Your Savings Cushion?

Concept

This activity establishes the importance of savings in relation to economic stability, another basic financial management concept. Investigators will determine the importance of this in their own lives.

Instructions

Investigators can choose to work alone or in pairs, according to their need for privacy.

Sequence

This activity is sequenced in these ways:

- "My Life Now" mental model in this module
- Wealth creation in Module 4
- Importance of financial resources in Module 7
- Self-assessment of resources in Module 9
- Planning to build resources in Module 12

V. A. Activity: Calculating Your Debt-to-Income Ratio

Concept

Understanding the proportion of income dedicated to all major expenses is important information needed to plan for economic stability. This investigation also heightens the discomfort investigators might feel about their current circumstances and motivates them for change by providing a means of articulating why they want to change.

Instructions

Review the example in the workbook and determine if the investigators have adequate working knowledge of their own or their household's income and expenses. Younger or otherwise dependent investigators might need to complete this investigation after gathering information from home.

Sequence

This investigation is sequenced in these ways:

- Causes of poverty presented in Module 4
- "My Life Now" mental model in this module

VI. A. Activity: Personal Mental Model: 'My Life Now'

Concept

At the end of this module, investigators will create their own mental model of "My Life Now." The creation and title of this mental model are important. This is a mental model of how things are now in the individual's life. It's important because it's a personal baseline. This is the mental model people will use to examine their own lives. Many investigators will look at it and be dissatisfied. After all, they have already decided to make major changes as evidenced by enrolling in school. The mental model of "My Life Now" can be used by the investigators to see the difference between what is and what could be. In the *Investigations* lexicon this is called one's "future story."

Instructions

Note that title "My Life Now" doesn't use the word "poverty"; investigators might not identify with that label, and it is not our purpose to label anyone in the group.

Investigators may feel discouraged, sad, angry, scared, etc., after creating this mental model. This "pain" or cognitive dissonance is not inherently bad. Indeed, it can be a catalyst and motivator for change. However, it may still be useful to ask some questions that affirm the students' strengths and abilities, such as:

- *What keeps you going?*
- *What motivates you?*
- *What strengths did you find in your mental model?*

As you work through the sessions, encourage the investigators to update this mental model. Reinforce the concept of rethinking and revision ("rolling revision"). For example, investigators might not put predatory lenders in their mental model at first, but when they learn about them in Module 4, they might wish to add them. Perhaps they omitted school from their model; ask them if they want to add it.

Sequence

The "My Life Now" mental model is sequenced in these ways:

- The mental model becomes an abstract representation of life. It brings some structures and definitions to the experience of poverty. It is the foundation for the self-assessment in Module 9.

- In the process of change in Module 3 the term "concrete" represents "My Life Now," and "abstract" represents new knowledge.
- It tends to create motivation for change and is a catalyst for the stages of change (Modules 7 and 8) when investigators see the discrepancy between "My Life Now" and what could be—the future story that is beginning to develop.
- It relates to the resources one has and the resources one needs when developing a plan in Modules 7, 9, and 10.
- Investigators will need to keep track of this mental model (along with all the others they have created) because they'll be adding to it and referring to it frequently throughout upcoming sessions.

VII. A. Activity: Time Management (Where Does the Time Go?)

Concept

The ability to plan is critical for college success. Many under-resourced investigators were never taught to plan and/or have experienced repeated failures of plans due to lack of resources and multiple stressors associated with their environment. Planning, therefore, like mental models, is an integral part of the *Investigations* sequence. Just as in developing the mental models of poverty and "My Life Now," the purpose of this exercise is to sensitize the students to the concrete reality and objective details of their present circumstances. This time-monitoring investigation provides another personal baseline, illuminates positive and negative elements in their lives, and helps investigators conceptualize the degree to which they currently control their time and choices. This investigation highlights disparities that exist between how the students perceive their efforts and activities and what they actually *do* in a given day.

Instructions

Brainstorm strategies for remembering to fill out the Time Monitor sheets regularly so accurate information is gathered. Can the facilitator text or e-mail reminders to the investigators? Can investigators buddy up to support and hold one another accountable to this task? Can they write reminders to themselves and post them in significant places, wear a rubber band around their wrist, and so on?

Sequence

The Time Monitor is sequenced in these ways:

- This investigation provides a great deal of concrete information that might precipitate additional revision of the mental model of "My Life Now."
- The Time Monitor also will be used in the planning exercise in Module 3.
- The Time Monitor provides information for investigating the relationships that support or undermine academic goals. In addition, the Time Monitor relates to the hidden rules of time, destiny, and power discussed in Module 5.

Writing Assignments

Family History

Write your family history. Consider the following areas:

Part 1: Describe the kind of work your relatives did and the education your relatives obtained.

Did they work "for" someone? Were they self-employed? What kind of compensation did they get? What level of education did they/do they have?

Part 2: Explain how work influenced the education they had—and how the education they had influenced the work they did.

During certain periods of time, there were places in America where a person could earn high wages with little education. There also have been times when people with a lot of education couldn't find work. (These, of course, were the exceptions.) Trace the relationships between education and work among your family members.

Part 3: Describe a vision for your college experience and the future.

Conclude your paper by describing the kind of education you want—and what kind of work you see yourself doing in 5 or 10 years.

MODULE 3

A Process for Change

Concept

Change is a theme throughout this book, as it is in higher education. Learning and using the process of change has the potential to free a person from the tyranny of the moment. Under-resourced students may have had experiences with hidden agendas and coercive tactics intended to "encourage" or "enforce" change by social service agencies, and they may experience some feelings of resistance upon entering the middle-class world of higher ed. Investigators continue to use their personal stories to articulate how change occurs. In poverty, the tyranny of the moment is about reacting to concrete problems with concrete solutions. *Investigations* teaches students to think abstractly about concrete problems, *then* develop concrete plans to solve them—and eventually, concrete plans to proactively prevent problems and achieve goals and to feel comfortable in this new environment. This process provides for emotional detachment and distance from personal issues needed to make informed decisions. This module explores *Investigations'* process of change because students need to know what the course is based on in order to be in a position of power and control. The exercises and discussions in this module are designed to open the topic of change, to make change relevant, and to make it something worth thinking about and acting upon.

Sequence

Change, the process of change, and the process of using abstract information to analyze and come to understand concrete experiences in a different way are central themes of the workbook. Module 4 provides an opportunity for an immediate change for a concrete problem—extracting oneself from relationships with predatory lenders and the like. Change through the use of language and negotiation appears in Module 6, and resources that support change, such as motivation and persistence, are presented in Module 7. Module 8 investigates the stages of change and, from that point forward, investigators evaluate their stage of change on a regular basis. In terms of the planning sequence, investigators assign abstract meaning and new definitions to describe how they spend time. Knowledge and use of the process of change can keep investigators focused on their future story in the midst of chaos; it is the stabilizing factor.

Learning Objectives: Investigators Will ...

- Understand the difference between concrete and abstract thinking and identify examples of each
- Begin to quantify the effects of the tyranny of the moment and account for how much time it takes to solve problems when resources are low

- Explore change theories used by most social service agencies and institutions
- Investigate how they and others have made changes in the past
- Actively choose whether or not to engage in a process for change
- Take responsibility for their thinking

Mental Models Labeled

Investigators will do a revision of the Mental Model of Poverty, with the addition of names of agencies involved with various aspects of poverty. They also will review:

- *Investigations'* Process of Change
- *Investigations'* Process Triangle
- Stephen Covey's Four Quadrants of Activity

Activities

I. A. Activity: Examining Agency Approaches to Change

Concept

The exercises invite the investigators to examine how most agencies and institutions address change. This shifts the conversation from the concrete (what did she say? how are we treated?) to the abstract (what are the theories behind the agencies' processes?). This is followed by new information about how people like or don't like to change—the personal side of the topic.

Instructions

Anchor the concept of "rolling revision" by revisiting both the group's Mental Model of Poverty and the investigators' personal mental models of "My Life Now." Add new information, concepts, and analysis to the models. The mental models become better, more detailed, accurate and inclusive with each revision.

Sequence

While in school, most investigators will probably continue to interact with some social service agencies. They can use this information to understand how to better negotiate with agencies.

III. A. Activity: Deciding to Change

Concept

Helps investigators think abstractly about the changes they have observed in others and in themselves.

Instructions

Keep this discussion relatively short to allow time to build the mental model in the next activity. Much of this work could be done in the journal.

Sequence

Examining the processes they have used in the past will help inform the strategies they choose to employ in the future, especially in Module 12 when they write their Personal Plan for Building Resources.

IV. Process of Change Mental Model

Concept

The mental model of the Process of Change will be useful in two ways. First, it will help investigators realize what happens in this workbook: People move from the concrete (the tyranny of the moment) to the abstract and a new future story. Second, it will help manage the group discussions, which can very easily get stuck in story telling.

Instructions

It's important that you as the facilitator draw the mental model that you see two pages hence as you describe the process of change. It would not be effective to make copies/handouts of this model; it must be drawn as you go to reinforce the active, intentional movement of the thinking under way. You also will want to save this drawing in the group's collection of mental models so you can refer to it as needed. *Detailed instructions for drawing and describing the process of change are found on the next few pages.*

This mental model will help you and the group *think* about the progress being made. You will likely find that the investigators have a lot to talk about because so many things can go wrong in the course of a week. The mental model can be used to show how, if we stay fixated on the problems of today, we will have a very hard time getting to the new information. It is a way the investigators can monitor themselves and keep moving through the material. If the group gets stuck in story telling, refer to the mental model and ask:

- *Are we getting to the new information?*
- *Are we able to let go of the problems of today enough that we can work on the content of today's investigation?*

You also might keep a running list of "Problems that make it hard to get out of poverty" as described in the section on teaching and learning. Thus you can both honor the experience of the investigators and also illustrate the differences between concrete and abstract thinking—and keep the processes moving forward.

Finally, be alert to how investigators shift from the concrete to the abstract and comment on it. Students will be learning metacognition—how to *think about one's thinking.* The first time this might have happened is when the group investigated the percentage of income spent on housing and began to summarize findings about the Mental Model of Poverty. That is working in the abstract. Recognize and encourage it.

Sequence

The Process of Change mental model is a foundational piece of the process in the workbook, as noted above. The labels or lexicon being developed provide a shared understanding of this new material so that the group members can proceed in developing a framework of ideas to apply within their individual and community plans. The activities in Module 2 that preceded the creation of the "My Life Now" mental model create cognitive dissonance, a discrepancy in the mind of investigators between what is and what could be. Future modules will provide an opportunity to resolve the dissonance, but for a time most of the investigators may be in an uncomfortable space. This Process of Change mental model cannot be developed without having first done the "My Life Now" mental model at the end of Module 2. The process of change is sequenced to resource development in Modules 7 and 10, as well as to the plan in Module 12.

It's all right if some investigators don't fully grasp the process of change the first time it's discussed because this concept will be reinforced in future discussions. The investigators will eventually teach each other this concept. One of the benefits of sequencing in this way is that the facilitator doesn't have to "hit a home run" with every concept the first time it's introduced.

Here is a step-by-step procedure for developing this mental model:

1. Instruct the investigators to draw this mental model, along with you, in their three-ring binders or journal.
2. Draw the inner circle and label it "My Life Now." This represents the mental model that each person drew of his or her own situation. Next, label this as "Concrete," meaning it requires people to solve immediate problems all day long and doesn't give them much opportunity to take on abstract issues. Explain that this is where we often get stuck. This is the tyranny of the moment. Many alcoholics, for example, repeat their experiences over and over, finding a way to get high, getting high, getting in trouble, getting over getting in trouble, and starting over again. (This discussion reinforces the learning from Module 2 that you just completed.)
3. Draw the outer circle and label it "Abstract." This is new information (what we intend to discover in this course), education (new ideas), and emotional detachment (when we can see our problems from "outside"). It's easier to go to this space when our lives are stable and we don't have large numbers of daily problems—or when there is time and energy for new things. To get out of the tyranny of the moment and to change our lives, we must be able to get to the abstract.
4. Draw the set of rectangles (representing plans) and the three lines (representing procedural steps), making the point that when resources are low, people need concrete solutions. Label this "Concrete Plans." When the electricity has been cut off, we aren't interested in budgeting information as much as we're interested in getting the heat and lights back on. Guide a discussion about how immediate concrete solutions often aren't effective long-range solutions. We have to get into the abstract to really solve our problems by detaching—and by using new information to develop new ideas or solutions.
5. Describe how unstable, under-resourced environments require that people use reactive skills to get concrete solutions to concrete problems. Draw an arrow from the word "Concrete" in the center of the model to the word "Concrete" beside the symbol for planning to illustrate how people go to agencies and friends to get those concrete needs met. Point out that there isn't time for the abstract when one is in crisis mode. Now draw a line from the word "Concrete" in the center to the word "Abstract" to illustrate how a person can choose to think in the abstract even during a crisis. Then draw a line from "Abstract" to the word "Concrete" beside the plan. This illustrates that a plan including *new information* will produce a solution that can lead to a completely *new direction* in life. When stuck in the tyranny of the moment, people are forced to solve the same problem in the same way over and over. *This process of change is the key to increasing economic stability.*
6. Now add the abstract concepts presented in *Investigations:* economic realities (the Mental Model of Poverty and the research on the causes of poverty), the stages of change so we can track our own success, and Payne's information (resources and hidden rules of class). This is the same information that is in the Triangle, an *abstract* representation of

what happens during *Investigations*. This information sequences back to the first day of class, as well as to the syllabus.

7. Write the word "PLANS" into the set of rectangles and "Procedural Steps" for the three lines below. This is where we begin to emphasize the value of planning and lists, which will be explored in greater detail in Module 4.
8. Now talk about how people move from the inner circle to the outer circle, how they cross that thin line. In other words, how do we, when we are stuck in crisis, find a way to detach so we can think abstractly? The investigators' workbook already has offered three ways this can be done:
   a. By developing mental models: As we learned in Module 2, mental models can help us see the big picture, connections, relationships, and options—all without a lot of words.
   b. By developing social capital: The second way is to have someone (like the facilitator) who can make the information relevant because he or she knows how to use the hidden rules of class.
   c. By using a mediated process (the way of this workbook): By investigating the *what* (past and present); the *why* (new information, including the disparity between what is and what could be); and the *how* (envisioning a new future story and developing a plan to get there).

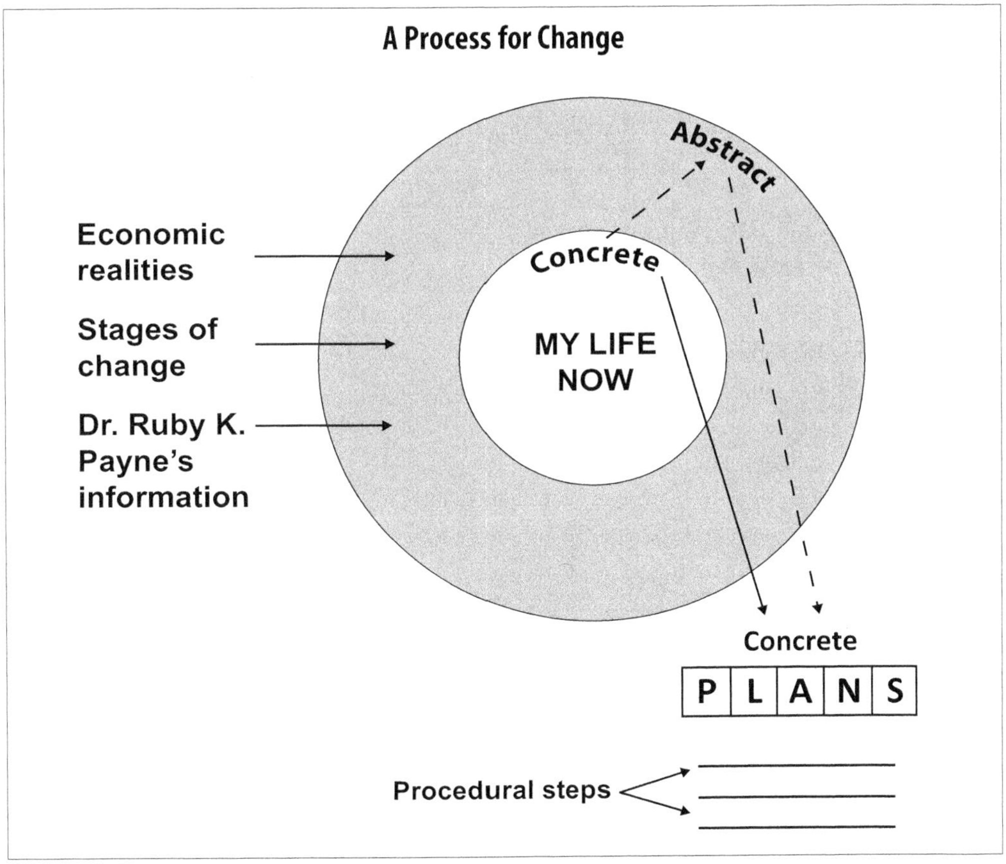

V. A. Activity: Time Management—Becoming More Effective

Concept

The conventional wisdom about study time is that, for every hour of class, students are supposed to spend two hours studying outside of class. So a student taking 12 credit hours is to study 24 hours a week outside of class. Whether an individual student needs to spend more or less time studying is up to the individual, but the point is, where exactly, will he or she find the time? This investigation puts students in the position to judge what is important and analyze how they might choose to spend their time—in contrast to how they actually have been spending their time. This investigation looks at a concrete problem abstractly, and it results in a concrete plan to solve it.

Instructions

Avoid the "righting reflex," which manifests itself in the temptation to tell investigators what's important, how they *should* spend their time, or why they *shouldn't* spend time doing such and such with this or that individual. Reinforce the ways an academic calendar helps with backwards planning. (See Appendix D for tips on student organizing, including the use of three-ring binders.)

Sequence

Using information generated from previous work, investigators practice going to the abstract and creating a plan. Next week plan to check back to see how well they were able to execute their plan.

Additional Notes

Campus Resources

It is likely that most of the investigators are unaware of student services on campus that might help them with housing, childcare, healthcare, counseling, etc. The temptation to provide this information is part of our own righting reflex. Investigators will look into campus resources later. For now, connect students to services on a case-by-case basis.

Notes on Organizing for Class

Confirm that investigators are keeping their materials organized and work with anyone who is having trouble.

One of the most common and pressing needs expressed is where to get cheap, used computers and how to learn to use them. You might want to investigate what resources are available to your students. A lack of access to computer technology can be a major barrier to success at the college level.

MODULE 4

The Rich/Poor Gap and How It Works

Concept

This module offers a theoretical foundation about economic class and an approach to analyzing solutions to poverty, as well as considerable factual information about income and wealth distribution in the United States. Our main purpose in exploring the causes of poverty is to illustrate that poverty is about more than the choices of the poor. There are many things that contribute to poverty over which individuals in poverty have little or no control. When students can recognize what *is* and what is *not* within their control, their emotional reactivity is lessened, and their ability to assume and assign responsibility for actions—their own and those of others—improves.

A broader view of the causes of poverty allows for analysis of solutions to poverty—a way to analyze policies and programs put forward by legislators and social service organizations. The discovery that ending poverty requires strategies for all four areas of poverty research leads to the realization that cooperation is necessary among individuals, community organizations, leaders (including the business community), and public policymakers. These insights help prepare investigators to participate in larger planning processes in the community and/or institutions.

Mental models of middle class and wealth provide information students can use to interpret the communication and behaviors of institutional staff (within social service agencies and colleges, for example). Investigators can choose their approach to others based on their analysis of the other *persons' mindsets.*

Sequence

New knowledge regarding the causes of poverty promotes abstract thinking about the Mental Model of Poverty and "My Life Now" mental model from Module 2—and supports the development of personal power and choices. An understanding of the differences in poverty, middle class, and wealthy environments supports the investigation of the hidden rules of economic class in Module 5.

This module is another point in the sequence when investigators begin making their own arguments for change as discussed in Module 3—and as will occur again in Module 8. They are starting to shape a future story for themselves in which they play a role in the community discussion, which is further explored in Module 10.

The planning sequence now offers tools for abstract analysis and intentional planning behaviors that reduce the need for concrete, reactive problem solving. The exercise regarding predators can have an immediate, positive economic impact, while the continuation of the time-management sequence offers a way to increase power over one's own habits and actions.

The first in a sequence of three optional activities that examine the issues of race, normalization, and discrimination is introduced because race is so closely intertwined with how wealth was created and passed on in this country. The first activity, which looks at the concept of normalization of the dominant culture, would precede the other activities included in the workbook.

NOTE: Module 4, as well as Modules 5–7, can be the foundation for development of long-term assignments, projects, or papers appropriate to credit-bearing courses. While some suggested readings are offered, there are many more discipline-specific readings related to economic class to support student investigations. In addition, Module 11 suggests autobiographies related to economic class, which can be examined for the presence of the concepts presented in *Investigations*.

Learning Objectives: Investigators Will ...

- Increase their knowledge about the causes of poverty
- Understand the mindsets and environments associated with different economic classes as a way of understanding the processes of change used by agencies and institutions
- Identify the personal and societal effects of economic class
- Identify a range of strategies to address poverty in the community
- Develop strategies to protect oneself from predators and to manage one's use of time
- *Optional:* Identify examples of normalization and daily barriers caused by racism and understand the meaning of societal issues, systemic discrimination, social bias, and the normalization of cultures; also develop new insights into their own experiences and the experiences of others, related to racial identity

Mental Models Labeled

- Mental Model of Middle Class
- Mental Model of Wealth
- Community Sustainability Grid

Activities

Optional: Systemic Racism

NOTE: This exercise (Valenzuela and Addington, 2006b) does not appear in the *Investigations* workbook. It is presented here for optional use.

Concept

Though there are many individual characteristics that intersect with economic class (gender, religion, etc.), none has as much impact on individuals, communities, and societies as does race. Race/racism is so inexorably linked to economic class that it must be addressed directly as its own category. The sequence shows racism as an embedded reality in society and underscores the importance of intentional strategies to confront and overcome it.

According to Becker et al. (2009), race as it pertains to economic class is a reservoir of hidden rules and resources. Race "is first explored metaphorically through analysis of the [systemic] bias toward 'right-handedness' of modern society and what it does and does not mean to the dominant (right-handed) vs. the oppressed (left-handed) cultures (Valenzuela & Addington, 2006b)" (p. 176). Investigators explore how *normalization* affects both individuals and society. The strategy of moving between our two story lines—the personal and the political, the individual and the societal—provides a means to process complex theories that may have had profound personal impact on each student.

> The discussion surrounding the personal, cumulative effect of race on the individual may shift the perception of the students who are white with regard to what the students of color have [experienced] and will continue to experience, regardless of their income or wealth. (Becker et al., 2009, p. 177)

This activity is an introduction to the concept of systemic issues. It's important to be clear that these sessions are not about enabling investigators to understand or deal with multicultural diversity. We presume that in order to develop a genuine appreciation for and skills in dealing with diversity, we have to first understand systemic racism.

Instructions

Please review Section III. on the facilitator's role as someone from the dominant culture.

Use this information to start off Module 4, before the section on the Research Continuum. It helps investigators understand what we mean when we say something is systemic or embedded in our society.

Activity: 'Handedness'

Introduce discussion about "handedness" by asking: Do we have any left-handed people in the room? Raise your left hand if you're left-handed.

1. **Explore our social bias for right-handedness**

   Lefties, would you say that our society is biased for right-handedness? What are some illustrations? (Get out several illustrations of our bias—scissors, notebooks, guns, cars, etc. Ask left-handed folks to talk about their experience with this bias. If there are no lefties in the room, then the right-handed people also should be able to illustrate. The facilitator should be prepared to help the process.)

2. **What is the significance of these daily inconveniences/hassles?**

   What do these daily inconveniences/hassles tell us about our society? What do they mean? (Encourage discussion of this question.)

   Analysis: These examples demonstrate how we have normalized right-handedness in our society. These daily inconveniences are not simply manifestations of our individual, personal prejudice against lefties, are they? It doesn't mean that the right-handed folks have something against left-handed folks. They are the effects of us having normalized right-handedness over a period of many generations. That is, being right-handed is the norm and being left-handed is different. Many things we use and even things we do are based on right-handedness. We shake hands or take an oath with our right hand. Even though in recent years there have been signs of greater sensitivity to lefties, it remains the case that right-handedness is the norm in our society. (Share illustrations and further explanation as necessary—such as the fact that the architectural standard for design is a 6-foot, right-handed male.)

3. **Handedness—a systemic feature of our society**

   Analysis: Handedness illustrates what a systemic issue is. It's "built in" to our social processes and is expressed in the daily experiences of living. It's part of the way things are and how they operate. Another way to say it is that it's embedded in our society and institutions. Right-handedness has been normalized; the challenges experienced by lefties are not simply manifestations of individual personal prejudice. Despite being more sensitive to individual differences, right-handedness is the norm. This illustrates a systemic issue—built into society, embedded.

Sequence

This activity is intended to lead into the rest of Module 4. This is the first of three items; the second appears in Module 5, and the third appears in Module 9. Module 12 provides an opportunity to conclude the sequence and integrate the information with personal plans.

I. A. Activity: Identifying and Detaching from Predators

Concept

Often investigators have not seen the payday lenders et al. as predators, nor have they investigated alternatives. Or, upon naming alternatives, they find them to be out of reach. Encourage the investigators to not only identify predators but to describe exactly how the predators work. Investigators use this activity to provide a concrete, immediate solution to an important problem.

Instructions

As a last step for this activity, introduce the concept of **backwards planning** to refine the individual plans to avoid predators. For example, if students intend to break free of payday lenders, they will have to pay off the lender. To pay off a lender, individuals have to know exactly how much they owe by what date. Then they have to know exactly how much income they will have by that date and what fixed or unavoidable expenses must be deducted from income available to pay off the debt. Then they will need a plan for how to fill the income gap—the difference between what is left after paying off the lender and what is essential for survival. For example, money for food could look like this: Eat at Mom's house Monday night, get to the free pizza party on campus Tuesday, eat at girlfriend's house Wednesday, super-size it on Thursday (saving half for the next day), and so on. Money for rent could look like this: Plan to pay rent late. Set aside late fee from next month's income (it will be less than the charge from the payday lender), call or meet with one's landlord to explain the situation, ask for one month grace period.

Sequence

The predator worksheet is important because it forms a specific list that can add accurate information to each individual's "My Life Now" mental model. This reinforces the concept of "rolling revisions" based on new information and insight. This activity also relates back to the mental model for the Process of Change from Module 3; predators exist in that portion of the model that is concrete and crisis-oriented and, as long as the students stay there, they will be at risk of being exploited.

Activities Contributed by UFE (United for a Fair Economy)

The following three investigations/activities—up to and including "The 10 Chairs" activity—have been contributed by an organization called United for a Fair Economy. The information about economic disparity and the causes of poverty is quite abstract. The mental models created through the UFE activities conceptualize the dry statistical data and create meaning and perspective. Have some fun with these activities to alleviate sometimes painful new insights. You will notice more detailed Instructions and Analysis items to support you and the investigators' use of these statistical and historical data. The following information is from *The Growing Divide* (2009), UFE's training manual.

II. A. Activity: Real Family Income Growth by Quintile and for Top 5%, 1946–79 and 1979–2006

Concept

This activity compares income distribution in two recent periods of economic growth in the U.S. Most people think they are "middle income"; it is often a revelation to learn otherwise.

Instructions

Props: It's helpful to have 8½ x 11" placards for each volunteer participant to hold, identifying the quintiles and showing the income range. (For the 1979–2006 period, see Step 4 on next page for the income amounts.)

To demonstrate both the growth and decline of incomes in these two periods, ask five volunteers to come up and stand in the front of the room. (For this activity to work well, the volunteers will need plenty of space to move forward and some space to move back.) It's important that the group focus on the top 1% to 5% of the population—the greatest beneficiaries of the growing divide. It's also important that all students get a chance to see where they fit in terms of income distribution.

Demonstrate the 1979–2006 time period *before* the 1947–79 period because our experience has shown the activity to be more memorable that way. It also gets investigators thinking about government programs that generally supported greater economic equality in the 1950s and 1960s (e.g., the GI Bill; appropriations for higher education, housing, and infrastructure projects; more favorable law enforcement; etc.). A suggested *facilitator narrative* follows.

1. We are going to look at the changes in family income during two recent periods of economic growth. First, let's talk a little about income. What are some examples of income? (Comments might include wages, salary, interest on savings account, Social Security check, rent from owning real estate, capital gains from selling investments, dividends from stocks, gifts, etc.) Now let's have five volunteers come to the front of the room. Please stand should to shoulder. (Hand each volunteer a placard showing the income range—in pre-tax 2006 dollars—of the quintile he or she represents.)
2. Listen to this introduction to the concept of income quintiles: Economists often talk about the U.S. population in "quintiles" or "fifths" of the population. They imagine the entire population of the U.S. lined up in order, from the lowest income to the highest. They then divide that line into five equal parts. This activity will look at what happened to the incomes during two periods of economic growth: 1947–79 and 1979–2006.

Let's look at some of the folks who are in these quintiles. What sorts of occupations or economic situations would you imagine fall into each quintile? Remember, this is family income. (A family is two or more related individuals living together.)

3. The following demonstration may seem like the childhood game "Mother, May I?" (also known as "Giant Steps"). Each volunteer, representing a quintile or fifth of the U.S. population, will step forward or backward according to whether his or her income gained or declined. Each step equals a 5% change—so, for example, two steps forward would indicate an income gain of 10%.
4. Between 1979 and 2006 here's what happened:

Quintile	Steps	Percentage Change	Yearly Income, 2006 (family income before tax)
Lowest	Baby step forward	+1.0%	$0–25,616
Second	2 steps forward	+9.5%	$25,616–45,021
Middle	3 steps forward	+15.5%	$45,021–68,304
Fourth	5½ steps forward	+27.0%	$68,304–103,100
Highest	11½ steps forward	+57.0%	$103,100 and higher

5. Watch what happens when we break that top quintile down even farther and look at only the richest 5% of the population. Rather than tear off the arm of our highest quintile volunteer, let's have another volunteer from the audience represent the top 5%—people with incomes of $184,500 and up. From 1979 to 2006, the income of this group grew 87.5%. (From the spot where the top quintile is standing, the sixth volunteer takes three additional steps forward—17½ steps in total from the starting line.)

Quintile	Steps	Percentage Change	Yearly Income, 2006 (family income before tax)
Top 5%	17½ steps forward	+87.5%	$184,500 and up

6. Watch this demonstration of what happened to the quintiles during the post-World War II years: 1947–79. We will start with the top four quintiles. This time (for space reasons), for every *10%* gain, the volunteer will take a step forward. How well (number of steps forward or backward) do you think the bottom quintile fared? How about the top 5%? What strikes you about these two periods in history?

Quintile	Steps	Percentage Change
Lowest	12 steps forward	+116%
Second	10 steps forward	+100%
Middle	11 steps forward	+111%
Fourth	11½ steps forward	+114%
Highest	10 steps forward	+99%
Top 5%	8½ steps forward	+86%

Analysis:

- From 1979 to 2006, there was much growth in income, but the distribution of that growth was very uneven. Although the top 20% as a whole did well, the ones who really made out were the top 5%.
- Why this skewing of income from 1979 to 2006?
- At the top, the biggest income growth source was income from assets (rental income; earnings from stocks, bonds and other investments; capital gains from sales of property and investments). Since asset ownership is heavily concentrated in the wealthiest 20%, it isn't surprising that this is where the gains went.
- There was explosive growth in CEO salaries.
- A weakened labor movement was less able to prop up the wages of workers at the bottom of the scale.
- At the bottom, the real value of the minimum wage was allowed to fall during the 1980s.
- From 1947 to 1979, incomes for each quintile as a whole—from top to bottom—basically doubled. In fact, the greatest increase was experienced by the bottom 20%. And the smallest increase was experienced by the top 5%. In other words, the divide between top and bottom in the United States actually narrowed slightly during this period.
- However, while the rate of income growth during this period was generally the same for everyone within each quintile—the significant gap between the incomes of African Americans and white Americans remained wide (see Family Median Net Worth by Race, 2004).
- Our purpose is not to glorify the 1950s but to point out that we achieved greater income equity across the quintiles. Also, the chart reflects the positive impact of social programs from the 1950s through the 1970s.
- The period from 1947 to 1979 demonstrates that the great disparity in the distribution of income growth, as happened from 1979 to 2006, is not inevitable. Rather, it is, in part, the result of deliberate government policies.
- The goal of the government during the early post-World War II period was to build a middle class. Programs such as the GI Bill—which allowed hundreds of thousands of returned veterans to go to college and purchase homes—were funded by relatively high taxes on the wealthy (the top tax rate was 91%). It is important to acknowledge that these programs disproportionally favored white men. For example, the Veterans Administration and Federal Housing Administration loan programs for housing, both of which utilized racially restrictive underwriting criteria, ensured that hardly any of the $120 billion in housing equity loaned from the late 1940s to the early 1960s would go to families of color. These loans helped finance more than half of all suburban housing construction in the country during this period, less than 2% of which ended up being lived in by people of color.
- The goal of the government since 1980s, however, was to let the rich accumulate great capital in the belief that it would trickle down.

II. C. Activity: CEO Pay as a Multiple of Average Worker Pay, 1960–2007

Concept

This activity dramatizes the widening gap between the highest paid workers in the U.S. and those with average pay. It explores why the wage gap in the U.S. is wider than in other nations. This activity is a role play that illustrates the ratio between chief executive officers (CEOs) and average workers.

Instructions

Props for this learning activity: Six placards that say: "Japanese Average Worker" ... "German Average Worker" ... "U.S. Average Worker" ... "Japanese CEO" ... "German CEO" ... "U.S. CEO"

Six volunteers, each carrying an identifying sign, will role-play CEOs and average workers from three different countries. The volunteers representing CEOs will move across the room in proportion to the difference between their compensation and their workers' pay. A suggested *facilitator narrative* follows.

1. Let's have six volunteers who will represent workers or CEOs from the U.S., Japan, and Germany line up in two columns facing the audience. One column represents the CEOs and the other column is average workers. *

   Please hold a sign identifying who you are so all can see. The U.S., Japanese, and German CEOs will move sideways step by step with each step equal to a 5-times ratio (therefore, if an average worker was paid $20,000 and the highest paid executive receives 10 times that amount—$200,000—then they would be two steps apart).

   The income ratio between the German CEO and the German worker is about 21 to 1. The German CEO takes four sideways steps. Next, the Japanese CEO—a little less than the German CEO (9 to 1): two sideways steps. In the U.S. the ratio is 44 to 1: nine steps.

* These comparisons are for industrial corporations with sales of approximately $500 million, surveyed by the Towers Perrin consulting firm in 2004.

   U.S. worker and U.S. CEO (9 steps)
   Japanese worker and Japanese CEO (2 steps)
   German worker and German CEO (4 steps)

2. Now if we look at the 365 largest U.S. firms as reported in the Annual Executive Pay report by *BusinessWeek,* in 1980 the ratio of CEO pay to the average worker was 42 to 1 (eight steps apart). In 2004 the ratio was 431 to 1 (86 steps apart).

   U.S. worker (1980) and U.S. CEO (8 steps)
   U.S. worker (2004) and U.S. CEO (86 steps)

Analysis:

- CEO overcompensation hurts average Americans. It transfers wealth upward from employees and shareholders to already affluent top executives.
- Organizational management consultants, such as Peter Drucker, believe that corporations must flatten out their structures, which exist primarily to justify excessive salary differentials. He speaks specifically of establishing a wage ratio between top and bottom.

- In recent years, shareholder activists have sparked public attention to the issue of the huge gaps between CEO and worker pay. More than 350 resolutions on executive compensation were filed in 2007. Whole Foods Market set a positive example by limiting CEO John Mackey's salary to no more than 14 times the pay of the average frontline employee. Contact UFE for more information about shareholder campaigns for pay equity.
- Angelo Mozilo, CEO of Countrywide Financial, earned $102.8 million in 2008. That means he made $1,976,923 a week … $282,418 a day … $35,302 an hour. He earned 90 times the minimum hourly wage every *minute!* His compensation is about equivalent to 3,000 well-paid account managers. Because of the cap on wages that are subject to the Social Security tax, Mozilo was done paying into Social Security at 1 p.m. on January 2, before the end of his first day of work. Most of us saw money taken out of every one of our paychecks.
- Some CEOs win big when their company outsources jobs to low-wage countries, such as India. Despite the claim of former Bush administration economic adviser N. Gregory Makiw that outsourcing is a "good thing" that boosts efficiency and profits that will support jobs in the U.S., there is no evidence to support this. Outsourcing does indeed increase profits, but they appear to be going into the pockets of chief executives. Of the 50 leading services-outsourcing firms, their CEOs received on average a 46% increase in total compensation in 2003, compared with only a 9% pay raise for the average CEO, according to *BusinessWeek.*
- Also of note is that the CEOs of the 69 publicly traded U.S.-based corporations that were listed as financial or in-kind sponsors of the two major political party conventions in 2000 enjoyed a 52% increase in average pay, compared with a 9% increase for the average CEO.

II. E. Activity: Ownership of Household Wealth in 2007—'The 10 Chairs: the Difference Between Wealth and Income'

Concept

Investigators will define and compare the concepts of "wealth" and "income." By using humor and having fun, investigators will dramatize wealth inequality and the dramatic shift in wealth from 1979 to 2004 for the top 1%.

The first part of this activity (see Instructions on next page) establishes the difference between wealth and income so that participants will have a solid frame of reference as they experience the dramatic "10 Chairs" activity that follows. With a lot of time, the discussion about wealth and income can happen in pairs or small groups first, then a sample of responses can be shared. The 10 Chairs activity portrays the distribution of household wealth in the U.S. in 2004 between the top 10% and everyone else, compares the distribution of wealth for the top 1% in 1976 and in 2004, and engages participants in dialog about wealth inequality. It works best with chairs that do not have arm rests. The chairs can be lined up across the front of the room facing the participants, prior to the start of the activity. Each chair represents 10% of all the private wealth in the United States. Each of 10 volunteers represents 10% of the population of the U.S. It is helpful to identify one student who is willing to represent the "top 10%" who may have a sense of humor or theatrical qualities (i.e., a "ham"). This activity strives for dialog between the trainer and the volunteers in their roles, as well as dialog and reflection among all the investigators. Remember to encourage a round of applause for all the volunteers at the end of this activity. A suggested *facilitator narrative* follows.

Instructions

1. First let's listen to a standard (economist's) definition of wealth (see the first Q&A in the box below).

   Name examples of assets that low-income, middle-income, and upper-income people might have. (The facilitator can note that there are other ways to view wealth, and participants can be asked to share alternative definitions, e.g., "A person can be considered rich in education, experience, influence, children, etc.")

2. Let's have 10 volunteers stand in front of one of the chairs. We need one person who is willing to be the "top 10%." (Remember to try to select a person who is a bit of a ham.) Each person represents one-tenth of the U.S. population, and each chair represents one-tenth of all the private material wealth in the United States. If wealth were evenly distributed, this is what it would look like—one person, one chair.

What Is Wealth?

Question: How is wealth different from income? What is wealth?
Answer: Wealth is private assets minus liabilities (debt). Simply put, wealth is what you own minus what you owe. Income is your paycheck or government benefit check or dividend check—or your profit from selling an investment. Wealth is what you have in the bank and the property you own.

Question: Is it possible to have negative wealth?
Answer: Yes. Seventeen percent of the U.S. population in 2004 had no assets, or they had negative assets: They owed more than they owned.

Question: What are examples of assets that lower income people might have?
Answer: Cash (checking and savings accounts), furniture, a car.

Question: What are examples of assets owned by middle-income people?
Answer: Cash (checking and savings accounts), equity in a house, a small business, some stocks, and/or a retirement fund.

Question: What are examples of assets owned by the top 1%?
Answer: Real estate, large stock and bond holdings, businesses, and paintings and other collectibles.

3. Currently (the most up-to-date data we have come from 2004) the top 10% owns 71% of all private wealth. The volunteer representing the top 10% takes over seven chairs, "evicting" the current occupants and making himself or herself comfortable on their expanded share of the wealth pie. The rest of the volunteers (representing 90% of the U.S. population) must share three chairs—or about 30% of the wealth pie. (This may require some shepherding and encouragement. Groups less familiar with one another will cluster, sitting and standing around the chairs.)
4. Even within the top 10% there is great disparity—a disparity that has increased significantly over the last 25 years. In 1976 the share of the top 1% was 22% (about two chairs). But by 2004 their share had increased to more than 34% of all wealth (3½ chairs). That's as big a piece of the wealth pie as the bottom 90% have combined! (To illustrate this, the facilitator can let the arm of the volunteer representing the top 10% represent the wealthiest 1% of the households, or you can use a top hat or other item of ostentatious wealth.)
5. Notice the circumstances you are in and your own feelings about this. How are you feeling at the top? How about in the bottom 90%? If you were going to push someone off the chairs to make room, who would it be? Why? What conclusions do you draw about the focus of public policy discussions—looking up the chairs (at the top 1%) or looking down the chairs at the disadvantaged? What questions do you have? Often folks direct their anger at the person representing the top 10%. Yet in reality this group remains largely invisible to the rest while wedges based on race, gender, sexual orientation, age, and class are driven between folks, and we all battle each other for more space on the few remaining chairs.

Analysis:

- Wealth is private assets minus liabilities (debt). Simply put, it's what you own minus what you owe.
- The shift in wealth (from 1976 to 2004) is an alarming one in so short a time frame (less than 30 years). Although the total wealth "pie" grew, wealth is now more concentrated in the U.S. than at any time since the 1920s.
- The share of private wealth owned by the top 1% now is more than the bottom 90% of the population combined. In fact, one man, Bill Gates, all by himself, has as much wealth as the bottom 40% of all the households in the United States.
- In 1982 the wealthiest 400 individuals in the Forbes 400 owned $92 billion. In 2004 the net wealth of the 400 richest people in the U.S. increased to more than $1 trillion!
- Too much wealth in too few hands fuels speculation, destabilizing the jobs and security of many people. Besides, there are only so many race horses, works of art, or face lifts any one person can have. More money in more people's hands would be a better fuel for the economy. As Randy Albelda, Nancy Folbre, and the Center for Popular Economics (1996) put it: "Mink coats don't trickle down" (p. 76).

- The shift in the ownership of income and wealth (and the changing nature of work) will likely hit the next generation particularly hard. Many young people who grew up in middle-class families may never have a standard of living approaching their parents—and therefore will increasingly be dependent on their parents' savings (equity) to help them build any security. Lower-income young people face the prospect of a lifetime of economic insecurity.
- Wealth begets wealth. The impact of compounding interest multiplies wealth for asset holders.

VI. A. Activity: Mental Models of Middle Class and Wealth

Concept

Now it's time to examine the economic environments associated with stable middle class and with generational wealth. Most investigators and many facilitators have never thought analytically about these economic environments and how they affect people's behaviors and interactions. These mental models complete the set of three economic environments.

Instructions

Investigators will be making mental models of what life is like for the middle class and for those from wealth. The activity calls for the investigators to read the stories and draw the mental models. You might divide the class into two groups, both tasked to create one of the mental models and present their findings for additional input from the group.

MENTAL MODEL OF MIDDLE CLASS

Analysis:

The Mental Model of Middle Class (above) includes key elements of the middle-class environment. The following might come out of the analysis: Stability, choice, problem solving, power, plans. Education as a driving force ties many elements together. Relationships are more interdependent and should increase stability and achievement.

MENTAL MODEL OF WEALTH

In the Mental Model of Wealth (above), the environment is generally so stable that people don't have to worry about work or what's going to happen today or tomorrow. Most of them are thinking long range, generations into the future.

Sequence

These mental models are important because you will be using them to illustrate where the hidden rules of middle class and wealth come from. These will become part of the group's collection of mental models. This also will be an opportunity to build a future story that includes all three classes (poverty, middle class, and wealth) working together to create a sustainable community.

IX. A. Activity: Backwards Planning

Concept

The short time horizon fostered by unstable economic environments affects the planning skills developed by investigators. You may encounter some students who don't own or use any type of academic calendar or planner. They may not relate the syllabus to the calendar. Learning and practicing basic planning skills related to a concrete upcoming assignment helps students ground the skill in relation to short-term needs. "Backwards planning" sums up the process of envisioning the end result, then working backwards to set intermediate goals or objectives by repeatedly asking, "What has to happen before that can happen?" Investigators become habitual in creating SMART (specific, measurable, attainable, realistic, time-specific) goals/plans to help them organize their time and complete assignments.

Again, avoid the "righting reflex" which manifests itself in the desire to have students develop more abstract plans for their future success. Development of a Personal Plan for Building Resources is the focus of Module 12 and beyond, when students will have more and better information to work from.

Instructions

Writing a plan to address one's involvement with predators is a very concrete planning task presented in Module 4. Other planning tasks depend on how the facilitator chooses to approach the variety of investigations in Module 4—and also whether the course requires outside assignments or projects to which the planning process might also be applied. If the investigators are not responsible for papers or projects associated with *Investigations,* they likely will have such assignments for other courses—or milestones to reach on the pathway to enrollment. Anchor the learning in the real-life goals of the investigators.

It's important to connect the plan to a personal academic calendar. From this point forward, require students to bring their calendar to each session. Refer to it each session, having students report on upcoming assignments in other classes or deadlines, special events, and so on. If resources exist, actually providing students with a planner bridges that gap. You may want to present it to them at the start of the course—or choose to wait till this moment when the group has stabilized and the deadlines and pressures of other coursework are beginning to motivate them to develop strategies to address assignments.

Depending on the needs of the class, the planning activity can be done by individuals or in small groups, or the facilitator might demonstrate the step-by-step process as it relates to some expectation of the course—a final paper, for example. Examples might include the task of learning about using the computer databases in the library. Students could develop a short-term objective and mini-plan related to building their Internet research skills; this may be a good time to introduce Internet research techniques.

Another example might include dates for a birthday party. This opens the door for a discussion of priorities and relationships. How can students account for their personal needs, such as their children, partners, or parents? Engage the students in the brainstorming about what steps must be taken, and encourage them to prioritize them by importance, indicating most important with the letter A, least important with C or D.

Sequence

The analysis of the Time Monitor information feeds development of detailed and precise plans that account for the complex interplay of factors students must manage. Students will continue to create backwards plans throughout the rest of the course. Students may already be recognizing the effects of positive and negative relationships on their plans. More about personal relationships will be discussed in Modules 5, 7, and 8.

Writing Assignment: Economic Class

Directions

Write an essay about economic class that has three parts.

Part 1: Define your own class position in American society, using our discussion and mental models of economic class to show how you fit into one (or maybe more than one) economic class.

Part 2: In the first part of your essay you've identified the social class to which you belong. Now, in Part 2, write about one thing you dislike about being in the economic class that you've described yourself as being in. As part of your explanation, provide one or two detailed examples that help your reader see precisely what it is you dislike about being in your class and why you dislike it. Keep the focus on only one thing you dislike.

Part 3: In the second part of your essay you've explained one thing that you dislike about being in your economic class. Now, in Part 3, write about a course of action that you can take to change this thing that you dislike. In other words, come up with a plan that addresses the problem that you identified in Part 2. Try to explain your plan in as much detail as possible. What, specifically, might you do?

Requirements

- Contains Parts 1, 2, and 3—as directed above
- Includes some meaningful discussion of material in the workbook or other sources
- Is organized into well-developed paragraphs
- Has been carefully edited and proofread
- Typed length: _____

Note. Adapted from writing assignments developed by Guy Shebat, English faculty, Youngstown State University, for use in "Getting Ahead Learning Community, 2008–2010."

Research Assignment: Issues and Causes

Directions

Choose an issue relating to economic class that is important to you (there are many examples of economic issues in Module 4).

This is a research paper. Research means you will have to find some additional sources of information to support your ideas. These sources of information should include at least three items from different sources, such as:

- Contemporary media (e.g., newspaper and magazine articles, interviews)
- Documents from businesses or agencies
- Books
- Internet sources

In this assignment you will write a six-part essay that investigates the issue you've chosen in relation to the four areas of poverty research, then write a conclusion about what you learned. You might use a blank "Community Sustainability Grid" to map out your thoughts and findings.

Introduction: Define the issue you have chosen and why it's important to you. How will understanding the issue help you?

Part 1—Choices: What individual choices do people make that contribute to this issue? Why do you suppose they make those choices? How do you account for their choices? What would make it possible for them to choose to do something different?

Part 2—Community: What in the community contributes to this issue—causes it, supports it, or provides opposition to it?

Part 3—Exploitation: Is exploitation involved? If so, who is exploiting whom, and why is it possible? If not, how do you account for that? Why is no one taking advantage of the situation?

Part 4—Policies: What policies influence the issue? These could be social policies, economic structures, or political policies that affect groups of people.

Part 5—Conclusion: Describe how Parts 1–4 connect with and reinforce each other. Discuss what might reduce the negative impact of this issue—and what might even cause the issue to be eradicated.

Requirements

- Discusses an issue from four different perspectives—research involving the four causes of poverty
- Shows how areas of research are connected to each other
- Is organized into well-developed paragraphs
- Has been carefully edited and proofread
- Typed length: _____

MODULE 5
Hidden Rules of Economic Class

Concepts

Hidden rules are the unwritten cues and habits of groups. These rules come largely from the environment in which a child is raised. In relation to economic class, e.g., the tyranny of the moment, as described by the Mental Model of Poverty, generates many of the hidden rules of poverty. Most of us, no matter what our economic class, know only the hidden rules of the class into which we were born—and maybe a few from another class. Knowledge of the hidden rules of middle class helps in navigating a world normalized to the middle class. Knowing the hidden rules of other classes is a tool for decreasing emotional reactivity and for fostering relationships of mutual respect across class lines. The eventual goal is for investigators to choose which hidden rules to use while building resources. An optional activity by Valenzuela and Addington (2006b) examines "Everyday Racism" and the barriers racism creates, along with the advantages it offers for whites.

Sequence

The process is moving from larger concepts created in early modules (Mental Models of Poverty, Middle Class, and Wealth; the floor plan; "My Life Now"; and the Covey activity quadrants) and drilling down into the rules, symbols, problems, and meanings associated with economic class. Students are moving from the cognitive style of story telling to (in this module) using the hidden rules to understand experience, behaviors, and environments, as well as to predict reactions. More words are added to the lexicon and ideas to the framework. New information is applied to personal situations and plans. According to Valenzuela and Addington (2006a), everyday racism provides a wider and more nuanced understanding of racism as an embedded, systemic reality that shapes everyday experiences—even without the clear presence of racial prejudice or intention (p. 4). The sequence shows racism as an embedded reality in society and underscores the importance of intentional strategies to confront and overcome it.

Although students haven't yet been introduced to the concept of resources (that comes in Module 7), it isn't too early to listen for the connections in their lives between hidden rules and resources.

For example, when an under-resourced student has trouble with a professor because of frequent absences or missed assignments, the student may react with anger to being informed of a consequence or attempt to deflect the tension by laughing. The hidden rules being used (either protecting personal reputation and relationships or being entertaining) actually work against building mental resources because they conflict with the professor's hidden rules of achievement and respect due to position. The relationship necessary for learning will suffer if the situation is addressed ineffectively. If the relationship is broken, the student's efforts to build mental (cognitive) resources might be derailed.

Learning Objectives: Investigators Will …

- Be introduced to and come to understand the hidden rules associated with economic class by applying them to current circumstances
- Use the "key points" to guide discussion about hidden rules
- Identify the mindsets of other people in relation to the hidden rules of economic class
- Develop skills in the use of hidden rules to build relationships of mutual respect
- Develop the confidence and self-assurance to express themselves in relation to the mindsets of economic class and the causes of poverty
- Discern the subtleties of systemic racism in everyday life and identify examples of the four features of racism

Mental Model Labeled

- Personal Mental Model of Hidden Rules of College

Activities

Information that follows may be helpful as you facilitate discussion about these ideas.

II. Key Points to Provide Perspective on Hidden Rules

Concept

As discussed in the sections about the teaching and learning process, this information can elicit various emotional and intellectual reactions, including resistance. The key points provide a tool to clarify the intention of the process, as well as reinforce individual power and choice.

Instructions

Ask the students:

- *Given what you have already learned about the three economic classes, yourself, and your community, which of these key points seem most important to you?*
- *Which resonate with other concepts we've explored?*
- *Are there any you don't understand?*

As the group continues to work, use the "key points" as a touchstone for staying grounded to the theory and process of change in this text. Often, if a strong debate arises, the key concepts can provide clarity and re-establish understanding.

Discussion on Key Point 11

In order to move from poverty to middle class or middle class to wealth, an individual usually must give up relationships for achievement (at least for a period of time). This key point begins a sequence that the instructor must attend to with care and sensitivity. It deals with a reality that almost every person encounters when he or she begins to move out of poverty; some relationships will change and others will be lost. The decisions that often have to be made about friends and loved ones can be very difficult. It's helpful to name this phenomenon so that the investigators have time to think it through and to manage the powerful feelings that this insight can generate.

Begin the sequence with the discussion questions on Key Point 11, but don't feel compelled to convince everyone to accept the idea. Group discussion will carry the concept to a certain point. You began setting up this sequence in Module 2 when the investigators created a mental model of the Floor Plan of their homes and named everyone who slept in their house. One point of doing that mental model was to think specifically of everyone who is close to you. The next time this idea can come up is in Module 7 when investigators create a mental model of Social Capital. That model helps identify how people who are bonding and bridging capital tend to support change differently. When the investigators begin to think of bridging social capital, they're starting to segue their thinking from the relationships they may lose to the relationships they may build. Touch lightly on this key point and allow the group to carry the idea forward. Finally, the sequence appears in Module 12 with the Support for Change mental model when the people who are likely either to sabotage or support change will be identified. At that time the investigators will be deciding who will be on their support team for the foreseeable future.

III. A. Activity: Studying the Hidden Rules

Concept

Students need this information in order to understand—from a less emotional, more intellectual perspective—their experience in society and the behaviors of people around them.

Instructions

Hidden rules stem mostly from the environment one was born into—not choice. At its worst, class distinctions can turn into judgmental statements and expressions of envy and contempt. Encouraging those who are most judgmental to take ownership of their experiences will have the intended effect of helping them develop their ability to suspend judgments while exploring the realities and experiences of other classes. The "left-handed" or normalizing exercise from Module 4 can be referred to here to help investigators better understand the meaning of being raised in a world that has been tilted toward the dominant group. Just as the physical environment has been designed for right-handedness, so has it been tilted toward the middle class, whites, tall males, Western Europeans, and people who use English in the formal register.

We suggest that you use the following pattern for studying each of the hidden rules:

- First, make sure you understand them. Investigate why the rules make sense for each class in each environment.
- Give examples of how the rules promote survival and elicit the respect of peers in each economic class.

Additional information about hidden rules

Time: We introduced the concept of the "tyranny of the moment" when we built the Mental Model of Poverty in Module 2, then talked about getting to the abstract in Module 3. Here you can make the point again that people who are stuck in the tyranny of the moment often think and talk about the present and the past but spend less time thinking about or planning for the future. On the other hand, some people in the middle class have a hard time being "in the moment" and enjoying daily life because they are so focused on future achievement.

When looking into the hidden rule for time, have the investigators draw several mental models for time. This reinforces the concepts of time and planning in this workbook. When you talk about time, it's helpful to draw a timeline that shows all three (past, present, future). Let group members come up with models of their own. One group used the "Slinky" as a model for time because of the ups and downs that occur for people in poverty. For example, it often takes students from a poverty situation four or more years to get through a two-year degree program because their environment tends to be unstable. Students from an economically stable environment are more likely to get through a four-year degree program in four years.

Possessions, personality, love, social emphasis, and power intertwine to affect how members of different economic classes experience relationships: In poverty, being "real" tends to be more important than education, degrees, and accomplishments. Individual personality is what one brings to the party. It's important to be entertaining, to tell stories, and to be funny. One woman told her kids, "We may not have money, but we're loaded with personality."

In poverty, *people* tend to be possessions. The more people you "have," the easier it is to solve problems. Connect hidden rules to the mental model of the Floor Plan of the house (and who sleeps where) and how multiple relationships are integral to solving problems. There's a lot of fear in poverty about family members leaving, including fear of young adults going to college. Acknowledge the existence and importance of relationships. Acknowledge that some relationships might change or even get let go when people try to start doing things differently (Key Point 11). Relationships can be a major barrier to change; students, however, likely aren't yet prepared to fully confront all that this means. Avoid belaboring the point. This issue is revisited again later when discussing change and future stories.

Sequence

This information provides opportunity for immediate action—and thus opportunity to analyze and process the results of such action. As part of the framework for understanding economic class, hidden rules repeatedly support investigations of personal and community resources, the building of plans, and consideration of the rules' role in executing the plans. There will be opportunities to reinforce how hidden rules can create either conflict or understanding, how they "make" or "break" relationships.

IV. A. Activity: Power and Public Policy

Concept

This simple exercise makes explicit the premise that those in wealth create policy, which is generally enacted by those in middle class upon those in poverty.

Sequence

Reinforces Module 3 discussion regarding agencies' agendas for change and suggests people from poverty might have a bigger role to play in policy and implementation.

Optional Activity: Exploring Everyday Racism

Concept

Utilizing the hidden rules of class, the video and discussion provide a means for investigators to further explore race and norms. By watching a documentary, investigators are able to identify racism and understand its pervasiveness as a systemic issue.

Instructions

On this page and the next are information and activity/discussion questions you may reproduce for investigators' use.

The video "True Colors" from ABC Primetime (Sawyer, 1991) is widely available in libraries. In addition, Justice and Witness Ministries has several copies of "True Colors" to loan out for short periods of time. JWM likes to keep the time to two weeks per copy.

Contact: Ferne Clements
Administrative Assistant
Justice and Witness Ministries
700 Prospect Ave., Cleveland, OH 44115
Phone: (216) 736-3725
E-mail: clementf@ucc.org

Also available from:
Employee University or
EmployeeUniversity.com/videos
(888) 215-8532
Item #5029
Purchase: $325; seven-day rental: $95
25% discount for education

Analysis: In "True Colors" John's and Glen's experiences clearly were not just illustrations of individual prejudice and discrimination. They illustrated something much more subtle, deeply embedded, and pervasive. Most of us who are white tend to be unaware of the many ways we benefit from the built-in biases that have normalized our racial identity. So now we need to deepen our exploration of these dynamics and relate them to our own experiences. A suggested facilitator narrative follows.

Everyday Racism

We've talked about the hidden rules of class. Now let's look at other hidden rules. We're going to explore racism as a systemic issue, like right- and left-handedness—and the ways it's present in everyday life. Recall some of the unvoiced expectations/assumptions that are expressed in the everyday experiences we mentioned that illustrate our bias for right-handedness. Racism is a similar kind of issue; it's embedded, built-in. But it's much more destructive than "handedness."

The video "True Colors" is several years old (it was produced by ABC-TV) and documents the experience of two professional housing testers from Chicago. ABC takes these two men—one black, one white—to St. Louis and puts them in situations where their experiences can be filmed and documented by hidden cameras. The program's producers intend to draw our attention particularly to the experiences of the black tester in order to demonstrate how race matters in our society.

Optional Activity: Video—'True Colors'

Time: 45 minutes for video and discussion
Materials: "True Colors" video or DVD and VCR or DVD player
Procedure: Your special assignment is to watch the white tester (John) and record all the advantages you see him receiving while the black tester (Glen) is routinely inconvenienced, hassled, ignored, and insulted.

Journaling, Discussion

- What scenes stood out for you? What do you remember?
- When were you most engaged?

- Did you have any emotional reactions? When? What emotions did you feel?
- What was going on in this video? What did it illustrate about racism?
- How does the video connect with the discussion on handedness?
- What did it illustrate about race and social norms?
- Based on your assignment above, list the advantages experienced by the white tester.
- What do these tell us about racism?
- Did any of this seem familiar—remind you of any of your own experiences?
- Who benefits in these daily experiences? In what ways?
- To what extent are most white people aware of these benefits and advantages?

Note. Adapted from *Systemic Racism: Daily Strategies for Survival and Beyond,* by C. Valenzuela and J. Addington, 2006b, St. Paul, MN: Minnesota Collaborative Anti-Racism Initiative. Copyright 2006 by Minnesota Collaborative Anti-Racism Initiative.

V. A. Activity: Hidden Rules of College

Concept

Colleges have their own unique environments and hidden rules for survival and acceptance within groups. Students need this information in order to understand that the focus on achievement through education relates to them personally and to feel comfortable capitalizing on the resources the college environment offers. The goal is for students to feel that the institution and its resources are indeed there for them—and to use this information to build relationships, thereby enhancing their academic career.

Instructions

These are good exercises to do in pairs or small groups, though each student might want to develop his or her own mental models. Add any particular hidden rules from your campus.

Sequence

As the group progresses, students will uncover additional information that relates back to this exercise. Encourage them to revise their models.

V. C. Activity: Hidden Rules of Financial Aid

Concept

Financial stress and lack of financial literacy, money management, and planning are major reasons students drop out of college. Aside from having low financial resources, the whole issue of money carries emotional baggage. Compound that with the highly abstract nature of financial aid, tuition, and the bureaucratic processes and language used to obtain it, and one can understand why so many students have trouble working the system to their greatest benefit.

Instructions

Inform the financial aid office that students are beginning this module and may be contacting them as part of their investigations.

Know that in order to complete the FAFSA—a prerequisite for any federal financial aid and the source of information most schools use to award scholarships—the student, if an adult, must have completed his or her income taxes. If the student is a dependent, he or she must have the income taxes for both parents. It is best to submit the FAFSA as soon as possible; the earliest date is January 1. The final deadline is June 30, but students who wait that long will miss out on many aid opportunities. NOTE: Parents who procrastinate on their income taxes cause delays in this process for their son or daughter.

If you choose to dispense information or advice in relation to financial aid, be sure you are knowledgeable and accurate. If you choose not to be a source of information, be sure to know where to refer students.

Sequence

Thus continues the process of building backwards planning skills with another concrete and relevant task—securing financial aid. This plan may be incorporated into the Personal Plan for Building Resources in Module 12.

V. D. Activity: Hidden Rules of Campus Social Life

Concept

This activity reinforces that students can learn and use the rules to build the peer support they need to succeed.

Instructions

These campus-related activities are conducive to being done in pairs or small groups. Investigators also might make the connection that the *Investigations* class has a certain set of rules and that the co-investigators are becoming a source of peer support different from any they have experienced in the past.

Sequence

As the group progresses, students will uncover additional information that relates back to this exercise. Encourage them to keep revising their models.

Writing Assignments

'Differentness'

Directions

Write an essay about "differentness" that has three parts.

Part 1—being "othered." Think about a time when you have had the experience of being "othered." What was the nature of the difference? How could you tell you were "other"? What hidden rules were at work in that situation?

Part 2—creating "others." Think of a time when you acted in a way that "othered" someone else. What was the nature of the difference? Was your behavior intentional or inadvertent? What hidden rules were involved?

Part 3—belonging. Think about a time when you participated in an event that made you feel proud of a group to which you belonged. What factors tied you to that group? What hidden rules were at work there?

Requirements

- Clearly describes the experience of being "othered"
- Includes hidden rules
- Is organized into well-developed paragraphs
- Is carefully edited and proofread
- Typed length: _____

MODULE 6

Language Rules and Resources

Concept

It is difficult to overstate the importance of language skills in college. There are many hidden rules regarding language, including registers of language, discourse patterns, language experience, story structure, voices, and mediation. Language skills are needed to negotiate and are specific to the workplace, whether to operate equipment in manufacturing, to be successful in knowledge sector jobs, to express oneself articulately in the service sector, or to give leadership to business startups, etc. Language creates the cognitive structures that create and store meaning and memory, it shapes and defines one's reality, it affects relationships and perception, and it precipitates both conflicts and resolutions. Becoming competent in language as it is used in different economic classes allows one to work comfortably with a diverse array of people. *Please review the Language section under Co-Investigation as a Process of Teaching and Learning in the* Facilitator Notes, *as well as Appendixes C and G1, for strategies to help investigators master and develop the content presented here.*

Sequence

Investigators continue the work of using hidden rules to understand their environment, experience, and relationships—and take action to build their own language resources. Language comes from our economic environment and is influenced by what we hear from parents and other adults, as well as the availability of and enthusiasm for books. Language skills also are investigated as a resource (in the next module), and they will be used by most investigators to build social capital and other resources as part of their personal plans developed in Module 12. The Ugli orange negotiation activity in this module reinforces the importance of both abstract and concrete knowledge that initially was introduced in A Process for Change in Module 3 (for example, while knowing about negotiation strategies is abstract, getting the specific information about what one is negotiating for is concrete).

Learning Objectives: Investigators Will ...

- Discuss five aspects of language: register, discourse patters, story structure, vocabulary, and voice—and explain why frequently there are language-related misunderstandings between classes
- Negotiate within middle-class institutions through the use of mediation skills
- Use formal register to express oneself, tell stories, and negotiate when circumstances call for Standard American English
- Identify concrete actions that will help children do better in school

- Identify the mindsets of other people in relation to the hidden rules of economic class
- Develop the confidence and self-assurance to express oneself in relation to the mindsets of economic class and the causes of poverty
- Develop skill in the use of the hidden rules to build relationships of mutual respect

Mental Models Labeled

- Formal Discourse Pattern and Casual Discourse Pattern
- Formal Story Structure and Casual Story Structure
- Mediated Learning
- Penance/Forgiveness

Activities

In this module, several summaries/overviews of information are provided, followed by discussion questions. In addition to the four major investigative activities (code switching, mediation, the Ugli orange negotiation, and a self-assessment of negotiating skills), some additional information—relating to language development in low-resource environments, with implications for college performance—is offered below.

Registers of Language

Formal register also is known as Standard American English (SAE). Martin Joos (1967) found that it is socially acceptable to shift one register in a conversation, but to go up or down two registers or more in the same conversation is usually considered inappropriate. Conversations in the casual register are supported by nonverbal communication.

Maria Montano-Harmon (1991) reports that, in order to move from casual register to formal register in English, students must actually translate word choice, syntax, and discourse patterns—skills that are rarely taught directly at any level. The upcoming information on code switching will address this issue.

Discourse Patterns

Discourse patterns are linked to how an individual gains access to language. J. P. Gee (1987) refers to "primary discourse" as the language a person first acquires and "secondary discourse" as the language necessary to function in the larger, or dominant, society. "Patterns of discourse—how information is organized for conversation—also relate to language registers. The discourse pattern in the formal and consultative registers is to linearly and logically get straight to the point" (Becker et al., 2009, p. 64). This is what is expected on campus.

> In casual register, … the pattern is circular and less direct. When under-resourced students attempt to explain a position, get help or direction, or express an opinion … in the casual circular fashion, they are often perceived as inarticulate at best and ignorant at worst. Similarly, when a person accustomed to circular, casual register discourse is cut short by someone … getting to the point, there can be misconceptions of rudeness or a lack of concern. (Becker et al., 2009, pp. 64–65)

Code Switching

Most children raised in poverty have only casual register English and are not proficient with SAE or formal register. Rebecca Wheeler (2008) refers to numerous sources that document how casual register causes incorrect assessments of students' actual reading, writing, and cognitive ability. In addition, traditional pedagogy that corrects "mistakes" in grammar and syntax for students who don't know formal register is basically ineffective in terms of actually helping students acquire the skill. That approach, coupled with negative attitudes and lower expectations on the part of instructors toward students' informal English, further depresses academic achievement. Wheeler cites 20 years' worth of linguistic research demonstrating that the patterns in casual register or informal English tend to be just as consistent as the patterns in formal register and hence are not *errors* in usage. She observes: "Students are correctly using the language patterns of their community" (p. 55).

Along with this insight come strategies to teach formal register language skills quickly, effectively, and respectfully. In an article called "Becoming Adept at Code-Switching" (2008), Wheeler spells out a classroom strategy called *contrastive analysis*. Contrastive analysis puts students in charge of an investigation of their own writing using the scientific method, which involves the following:

> ***Collect data:*** First, collect a set of sentences from student writing showing a particular sentence pattern.
>
> ***Examine data, seeking pattern:*** You'll then examine your student data to see what particular arrangement of words happens over and over and what meaning accrues to the pattern.
>
> ***Describe pattern:*** State in your own words what the pattern is.
>
> ***Test pattern:*** Make sure the rule you write out captures other data you encounter (Wheeler, 2008).

Once students have discovered and become conscious of their language patterns, they can *code switch* as a method of being intentional about their grammatical choices based on the circumstances, in the same way they become conscious of the patterns and use of the other hidden rules of economic class.

Contrastive analysis and code switching have been tested and proven highly effective (Wheeler, 2008). It should be noted that these strategies were written for and are used by elementary school teachers who have a range of backgrounds and are not necessarily language arts specialists—and generally not linguists. We encourage expanding use of this transformational strategy for college students and refer you to Wheeler's newest book, co-authored with Rachel Swords, titled *Code-Switching Lessons: Grammar Strategies for Linguistically Diverse Writers* (2010), for step-by-step instructions.

Given that not every facilitator will choose to engage in leading the contrastive analysis process, we offer an alternative activity that puts the learning into the hands of the investigators, using their own texts as sources of data and analysis. Please note that this approach cannot be considered contrastive analysis because it is missing key steps, and it has not been tested with college students. However, it does follow the pattern established in *Investigations* of putting the students in control of their learning and pointing them to additional sources of information.

III. A. Activity: Code Switching in Personal Writing Samples

Concept

Investigators use Wheeler's approach to analyze their own writing samples for the five most common differences in usage patterns between casual and formal register. Equipped with this information about their own language patterns and the code-switching charts for these five patterns, investigators can determine when and where to use different registers of language.

Instructions

Thus far, writing exercises in *Investigations* have been offered as optional assignments, determined in part by the nature and intent of the course. The critical nature of language register in relation to student success and engagement, however, requires specific and personal attention in the area of writing, as well as speech. If writing assignments have not yet been called for, and the investigators don't have writing assignments available from other courses, instruct them to write a paper—perhaps the assignment offered in Module 2.

Then have them analyze their writing for the presence of casual and formal patterns. They will compare their writing to the code-switching charts in *Investigations* and mark the usage patterns themselves. In your evaluation of their writing, refrain from using the words "errors" or "mistakes" or "bad English." Have students compare and contrast their samples with the examples on the code-switching chart and explicitly review the differences in the two language forms.

Finally, review the concept of *code switching*. First, students assess the circumstances. Who are they communicating with, for what purpose, where, and when? Which register or pattern is most appropriate given the circumstances and what they've been learning about language and hidden rules? "Because code switching requires students to think about their own language in both formal and informal forms, it builds cognitive flexibility, a skill that plays a significant role in literacy learning" (Wheeler, 2008, p. 57).

Sequence

This detailed investigation into hidden rules of language anchors the learning in the student's own writing and puts the power of choice and change in his or her hands.

Voices

Students who were raised in situations with limited parenting, those who had to take care of themselves and (often) their siblings as well, frequently have an overdeveloped parent voice and a weak adult voice. Given that conflict resolution and negotiation are largely predicated on the adult voice, these students can have problems establishing relationships and may manifest penance/forgiveness behaviors when confronted. The three voices (the child voice is the third) provide yet another way to label language usage that can accelerate learning.

Story Structure and Language Experience

Story structure affects more than just communication. Becker et al. (2009) note that cognitive and brain research shows that story structure is related to the way information is stored in the brain (Zull, 2002). Although casual stories might contain more information and be more entertaining, they are harder to process in terms of content and meaning.

Vocabulary

The proportionately smaller vocabularies of many under-resourced students can be built using research-based strategies. It is more effective to directly teach vocabulary and skills to build vocabulary, such as word consciousness and wide reading, than to spend time explaining or correcting misunderstandings. See Appendix D for additional strategies for building vocabulary.

Mediation

Explicitly teaching about mediated learning experience and reinforcing the components of mediation within the *Investigations* process will further ground this new knowledge in concrete application. For example, the Process Triangle that describes the syllabus in Module 1 and the process of change in Module 3 also encapsulates the *what,* the *why,* and the *how* of the entire course. The learning objectives at the start of each module summarize the *what, why,* and *how* of that module. Ask students to pick their favorite activity to date and categorize the components into the *what, why,* and *how* elements.

VII. A. Activity: Mediation in College Courses

Concept

One frequently hears students complain, "What does this (composition, math, history, etc.) course have to do with me becoming a nurse, electrician, or social worker?" The relevance of college coursework is rarely made explicit, even in professional/technical courses. Explicitly dissecting the mediated experience that supports the design of the *Investigations* course provides a concrete example of how to apply this information. Investigators are then asked to do two things—first, play with the language by translating the *what/why/how* of *Investigations* into less formal language, and second, define the mediated experience behind their other courses, which may require conversations with other instructors.

Instructions

Instruct students to "go to the text before them" and, sentence by sentence (perhaps even phrase by phrase), read aloud to each other and reinterpret in "ordinary" language. Depending on the demographics in the group, there may be some diversity in the language of the communities within which the investigators grew up, sparking comparisons of language patterns that relate back to the code-switching information.

You might discuss which hidden rules investigators can use when approaching other instructors in order to complete the second half of the assignment.

VII. C. Activity: Getting Time to Study Through Mediation

Concept

The brief activity included here can be helpful for students who also are parenting or taking care of other people's children. If investigators express feelings of anger or guilt about how they were parented—or about their own past parenting strategies—reinforce that they are learning new strategies and taking action to stabilize their environment, which is important not only for them but also for the children in their life. If few students are childcare providers, an alternative situation may be substituted.

IX. A. Activity: Negotiating for Ugli Oranges

Concept

Investigators can integrate all of the concepts they have learned—about language and other hidden rules through the activities—into methods to resolve differences. Investigators are using terms from the lexicon and connecting abstract ideas in complex ways. This activity teaches multiple aspects of negotiation and communication. Investigators take on one of two roles and receive information they can use to negotiate an agreement with the other party. Dr. Jones wants the juice from the orange crop, and Dr. Roland wants the rinds. They are both scientists working for rival companies and each wants the majority of the supply for a "good" (moral) reason.

Instructions

The student sheets describing Dr. Jones and Dr. Roland appear later in this module.

1. Read the instructions in the workbook aloud.
2. In pairs, have the students begin negotiating. Tell them you will stop them before everyone is finished.
3. If any students already are familiar with the simulation, ask them to help as your assistants to monitor the negotiations under way.
4. Stop the negotiations after 10–15 minutes or when approximately half the class has reached a conclusion.
5. Ask the pairs to report on their progress and the outcome of the negotiations. Usually half the class will be at *impasse,* and half will have some version of a solution, a compromise, or an integrative (win-win) agreement.
6. Review the Analysis below as it comes up in discussion of the negotiation process and outcome.

Discussion questions:

1. Discuss what made it difficult to find a solution.
2. Discuss what had to be done to find a solution.
3. When you are negotiating, how hard is it to see "the merit on the other side"?
4. Is "finding the merit" easier with some people than with others? Or in some situations compared with others?
5. What was the most important piece of information in the Ugli orange story?

Analysis: Everything is negotiable.

The most common approach is angels vs. devils perspective—a righteous cause, a win-lose situation, a zero-sum game.

Characteristics of the suboptimal agreements (50/50 compromise; 70/30 agreements, win-lose decisions)

- Used power or status ("I am with the government")
- Used seemingly rational arguments ("loss of adult life is worse than loss of infant life") to persuade the other
- *Answered the "why" question in the abstract (e.g., "I need the oranges to save pregnant women" vs. "I need the oranges to save infants") rather than in the concrete ("I need the juice/rinds to make the serum")*

- Engaged in "unethical" behavior while making agreements (e.g., one party offered the other negotiator a job if that negotiator "gave in" to the first party's wishes)
- Refrained from disclosure because of suspicions about each other "stealing" company secrets
- Allowed the stress of the hostile relations between the two parties to distract attention
- Allowed themselves to be threatened by the other party

Characteristics of those who reached no agreement

- Prior hostile relationship between parties prevented information exchange
- Information exchange was mainly for own priorities (e.g., what the other party will be bidding) rather than to come to an optimal agreement
- Although there was open communication, the personality of one party (selfish, arrogant, narrow focus) prevented parties from coming to an agreement
- Too stressed to listen to the other party's detailed communication
- Lack of trust because of prior hostile relationship
- Framed it as a moral dilemma: deaths of children vs. deaths of adults; which cause is worth more?
- Unethical behavior (deception and lying)
- Feeling of a "legal/moral" right (e.g., "I'm from the government")
- Time pressure prevented agreement

Characteristics of the integrative (win-win) agreements

The negotiation focused on interest vs. positions:

Position = I need all of the oranges.

Interest = I need the rinds/juice of all the oranges.

Both wanted to cure or prevent severe health problems.

Communication was effective:

- Recognized that information exchange is power
- Good questioning/good revealing

  For example: Why do you need oranges? What do you need them for? The specific question/specific answer is the key.

Note. Adapted from "MGTC24: Detailed Outline of Weekly Activities," n.d.

IX. F. Activity: Self-Assessment of Negotiating Skills

Concept

This activity asks the investigators to reflect on their knowledge of key concepts presented to date—and consider how well they think they could apply the information and skills in negotiations.

Instructions

Investigators can do this activity independently, then discuss their self-assessment.

The Ugli Orange Case: Student Sheet

Confidential Instructions to: Dr. Jones

You are Dr. Jones, a biological research scientist employed by a pharmaceutical company. You have recently developed a synthetic chemical useful for curing and preventing Rudosen, a disease contracted by pregnant women. If not caught in the first four weeks of pregnancy, the disease causes serious brain, eye, and ear damage to the unborn child. Recently, there has been an outbreak of Rudosen in your country and several thousand women have contracted the disease. You have found, with volunteer victims, that your recently developed synthetic serum cures Rudosen in its early stages.

Unfortunately, the serum is made from the Ugli orange which is a very rare fruit. Only about 4,000 of these oranges were grown in the whole world this season. No additional Ugli oranges will be available until next season, which will be too late to cure the present Rudosen victims.

You have demonstrated that your synthetic serum does no harm to the pregnant women. There are no side effects. Unfortunately, the present outbreak of Rudosen was unexpected and your company had not planned on having the serum available for six months. Your company holds the patent on the synthetic serum, and it is expected to be a highly profitable product when it is generally available to the public.

You have recently been told that a Mr. Cardoza, a South American fruit exporter, has 3,000 Ugli oranges. If you could obtain all 3,000 of these Ugli oranges, you could make enough serum from the juice of these oranges to both cure all the present victims and provide sufficient inoculation for the remaining pregnant women in your country. No other country currently has a Rudosen threat.

You have been told that Dr. Roland is also urgently seeking Ugli oranges and is also aware that Cardoza has some of these special oranges. Dr. Roland is employed by a competitor pharmaceutical company. Roland has been working on biological warfare research for the past several years. There is a great deal of industrial espionage in the pharmaceutical industry. Over the past several years, Dr. Roland's company and your company have sued each other for infringement of patent rights and espionage law violations several times.

You've been authorized by your company to approach Cardoza to purchase the 3,000 Ugli oranges. You have been told Cardoza will sell them to the highest bidder. Your company has authorized you to bid as high as $250,000 (U.S.) to obtain the juice of the 3,000 available oranges.

Before approaching Cardoza, you have decided to talk with Dr. Roland. Think carefully about what information you are willing to tell the other side and what information you will not disclose.

[*While you may tell the negotiators from the other side what is on this sheet, you may not show them this sheet.*]

The Ugli Orange Case: Student Sheet

Confidential Instructions to: Dr. Roland

You are Dr. Roland, a research biologist for a pharmaceutical company. Your company has a government contract to do research on methods to combat enemy uses of biological warfare, but the government has asked your company for assistance with an immediate problem.

Recently, several old experimental nerve gas bombs were moved to a small Pacific island. While they were being moved, two of the bombs developed leaks. The leaks are presently controlled, but government scientists believe that within two weeks the gas will leak out of bomb chambers and escape. There is no known method of preventing the gas from getting into the atmosphere and spreading to the coast. If the leak occurs, several thousand people will die or incur serious brain damage.

You have developed a synthetic vapor that will neutralize the nerve gas if it is injected into the bomb chamber before the gas leaks out. The vapor is made with a chemical taken from the Ugli orange, a very rare fruit.

You've heard that a Mr. Cardoza, a fruit exporter in South America, has 3,000 Ugli oranges. If you get all 3,000 Ugli oranges you could make enough of the chemical from the rinds of these oranges to neutralize all of the gas if the serum is developed and injected efficiently. Your company has not been able to locate any more of these Ugli oranges. As far as you know, there are only 3,000 such oranges in the world crop this year. You have learned that Dr. Jones is also urgently seeking to purchase Ugli oranges and that Jones is aware that Cardoza has oranges available. Dr. Jones' company and your company are highly competitive, and there is a great deal of industrial espionage in the pharmaceutical industry. Your company and Dr. Jones' company have sued each other twice for infringement of patent rights. One lawsuit is still going on.

You've been authorized by your company to approach Cardoza to purchase the 3,000 Ugli oranges. You have been told that Cardoza will sell them to the highest bidder. Your company has authorized you to bid as high as $250,000 (U.S.) to obtain the oranges.

Before approaching Cardoza, you have decided to talk to Dr. Jones. Think carefully about what information you are willing to tell the other side and what information you will not disclose.

[*While you may tell the negotiators from the other side what is on this sheet, you may not show them this sheet.*]

Note. From "Teaching Negotiation and ADR: The Savvy Samurai Meets the Devil," by J. Barkai, 1996, *Nebraska Law Review, 75*, pp. 748–750. Copyright 1996 by University of Nebraska. Adapted with permission.

Writing Assignments

Transformational Mediation—or Negotiation Meets the Process of Change

Read the short article below. Then write a paper that describes transformational mediation using the framework of the mediated experience (see mediation materials here in Module 6).

- What is transformational mediation?
- Why is transformational mediation important?
- How do you do transformational mediation?

Final Draft Requirements

- Uses the pattern of mediation to describe the elements of transformational mediation
- Is organized into well-developed paragraphs
- Is carefully edited and proofread
- Typed length: _____

'The Theme of Transformation in the Work of Carl Upchurch'

By T. L. Kelly

Introduction

The testimony of Carl Upchurch about his personal journey from being a gangbanger to becoming a national activist for peace, as chronicled in his book *Convicted in the Womb* (1996), is a clear example of how personal transformation can play a significant part in conflict resolution. Personal transformation is the basis for a relatively new theory of conflict resolution called "Transformational Mediation." Several ingredients go into the sort of transformations that work to resolve complex human problems, and it is the intent of this paper to deconstruct the process to discover those ingredients and give credence to the process of Transformational Mediation.

Stages of Transformation

The first ingredient that played into Upchurch's transformation was to be isolated from society and forced into a situation where he had few choices. He went to prison and was put into solitary confinement, where he had few choices as to how spend his time. Luckily for him, he found a book in his cell and began to read. The book was by Shakespeare, and in the reading of this and other works by Shakespeare, Upchurch was able to expand his own personal paradigm of thinking in an intimate, revolutionary way. His isolation, coupled with the discovery of a new way of thinking, worked as a sort of monastic meditation that led to personal enlightenment. In the final analysis, the ingredients in this stage of his transformation are isolation and enlightenment.

The next stage of Upchurch's transformation involved release into the world to put his "new self" to the test, just as monks are sometimes sent out of the monastery to participate in some aspect of the world in order to test their faith. In that test, Upchurch experienced failures and setbacks, which over time worked to strengthen his resolve and teach him humility. In a previous paper, I argued that failures and struggles are necessary to learn strength and wisdom in order to build character and conscience. Upchurch, grounded in his newly acquired enlightenment, learned humility and strength in this way, through these tests in the real world. This is when it became clear that education was an important ingredient to getting what he wanted from life, and so he sought a formal education, having been enlightened to its worthiness in his personal life goals. In the final analysis, the ingredients for transformation in this stage are trial and error, and education.

The final stage in this process is activism. Taking all the ingredients of enlightenment and putting them into action requires creative thinking and perseverance and even a bit of idealism. Upchurch came up with a creative action to aid the resolution of a complex human problem: gang warfare. The solution he used follows the stages of the process of his own enlightenment and transformation. He isolated gang leaders into one place and presented them with a clear challenge: stop the violence or die in violence. Isolated and faced with few choices, the gang leaders began the long, complex process of disentangling the web of violence in their lives. They had many differences among them, but they could all agree that violence had not solved any of their problems. Upchurch used the opportunity to educate those he had assembled, and to remind them of the true ingredients for the respect they sought—content of character and personal strength. He emphasized that there would be failures and setbacks along the way to transformation, having experienced the same for himself in his own journey. His words and actions were proof of the content of his character and his personal strength, which he had received from doing the same hard work he challenged the gang leaders to begin in their own neighborhoods. In the final analysis, the ingredient for this stage in transformation is to turn enlightenment into action.

Theory of Transformational Mediation

How does this relate to the theory of transformational mediation? Transformational mediation is a model of conflict resolution that values both personal strength and compassion for others, as well as viewing conflict as an opportunity for growth and mutual gain. The transformative mediator works to help the parties gain a greater sense of their own capacity to effectively deal with their conflict and an increased understanding of the other parties' perspective on the conflict. The hands-on version of this theory goes something like this: The mediator actively participates as a sort of alter ego for both sides, by literally circumventing the arena of the conflict and reflecting what is said back to the parties involved in order to narrow down the viewpoints to their root meaning. The mediator shapes the conflict dialog so that all parties become aware of the power issues and conflicts of meaning going in within the dialog. The parties in conflict not only work to resolve their conflict, they transform their view of the other, and realize the meaning and therefore the value inherent in the conflict itself. At the same time, the mediator realizes his or her role as an objective professional, not taking sides but revealing sides. The goal of this complex interaction is to promote enlightenment and transformation, not just negotiation and compromise. This form of mediation seems to me to be the type of conflict resolution that would complement the ingredients for enlightenment and transformation as discovered by Upchurch in his quest. It would be useful to compare Upchurch's methods to a model of transformational mediation for differences and similarities.

Note. Adapted from "The Theme of Transformation in the Work of Carl Upchurch," by T. L. Kelly, 2004, *New Tomorrow: A Voice for Blacks and Latinos.* Copyright 2004 by T. L. Kelly.

MODULE 7
Eleven Resources

Concept

In this module you will be introducing the core concept of resources, a foundational component of this work. This is where we define poverty and prosperity in a holistic way.

In this module we introduce one definition of poverty: "the extent to which an individual does without resources" (Payne, 2005, p. 7). Resources can be defined as quality-of-life indicators. It is also true that different people can value resources differently. Taking the 11 resources as a whole, it's safe to say it's better to have high resources than low resources. And it's important to note that while resources are far more than financial, it's fair to say that being financially stable reduces stress and allows for more choices.

Sequence

Up until now we have been co-investigating areas of research and hidden rules, which are systemic issues and generalizations. As much as they apply to our sense of identity and belonging, they are generally easier to talk about than one's personal resources. Although we have been using the word "poverty" for some time, the definition is anchored at the start of this module. People in poverty tend to have lower resources than others. This is made easier to understand in relation to the Mental Model of Poverty created in Module 2. Being poor in the U.S. means being vulnerable to daily fears and problems to the extent that one almost inevitably becomes trapped in the tyranny of the moment. There's not enough time or energy to solve daily problems, let alone build financial, emotional, mental, and social resources.

The concept of resources segues back to hidden rules because what people value and how important it is relates to the economic environment they came from. The information about change as it relates to motivation and persistence ties to Module 3 and supports the next module when stages of change are explored. The Resources Scoring Table in this module is the basis for the self-assessment that will be done in Module 9.

Learning Objectives: Investigators Will ...

- Be introduced to and come to understand the 11 resources
- Use case studies to practice doing assessments of resources
- Begin to evaluate their own social capital as it relates to support for change

Mental Model Labeled

- Mental Model of Personal Social Capital

Activities

Additional information related to resources is provided below to support facilitation of this module.

Emotional Resources

Emotional Intelligence

Students who have not been well-prepared academically might find previously unnamed strengths in the areas of emotional intelligence. The stress experienced in under-resourced environments frequently enhances individuals' ability to "read" *other people* and empathize with them. On the other hand, there may be issues related to difficulty in recognizing/managing *personal* emotions and controlling impulses.

Mental/Cognitive Resources

Learning Styles/Study Strategies

Students, particularly those in need of remedial reading and study skills, report that discovering their particular learning style was extremely helpful to them—both in understanding past experiences in schools (and self-diagnosing current academic hurdles) and in choosing more effective ways to study. Students not in a study skills-oriented course might investigate their options on campus. Finding non-credit programs to build skills saves students significant tuition dollars. The VARK (visual, aural/auditory, read/write, kinesthetic) Learning Styles questionnaire and study guidelines are available at *www.collegeforadults.com.*

Learning Disabilities

Many students may be affected by learning disabilities, whether diagnosed or not. The National Center for Learning Disabilities (NCLD) has useful information about the nature of learning disabilities, as well as a chart detailing the type of disability, the signs, and strategies to mitigate the effects of the learning disability (WETA-TV, 2010).

Social Capital

The information on social capital provides investigators with something they can act upon immediately. They can use their skill at building relationships to attract social capital—allies who can help them later as they implement action into their plans.

III. A. Activity: Mental Model of Personal Social Capital

Concept

This exercise focuses on two major types of social capital: Bonding relationships and bridging relationships. Bonding relationships provide reassurance that our behavior and feelings are OK, because the people we bond with tend to have the same ideas we do about things. They might be family or friends, but they are part of our personal group that supports the norms and values shared by the group. Bridging relationships, on the other hand, involve connections with people not like ourselves who give us access to information and opportunities we otherwise likely wouldn't have (Putnam, 2000).

Instructions

A number of students might come to the realization that some of the relationships in their lives are not supportive—or are even destructive or toxic. This can be frightening and saddening, especially if the relationships are with close family or have endured a long time. Watch for student reactions that can range from "aha" insights to emotional devastation. If their reactions are more intense than is comfortable for you, show support, then link them to counseling resources on or off campus.

As the instructor or facilitator of the group, you are *de facto* bridging social capital. Your students might be bridging social capital for you as well. If you are from the middle class, your students might provide you with access to people from poverty whom you can learn from. They can share inside information about their families and communities that you would not have access to otherwise. They can provide you with a sounding board to test out new ideas about how to approach this work—and perhaps even assist, in effect, with lesson plans for other courses you teach.

Sequence

Social capital is assessed directly in this module; specific plans for building social capital will be addressed in Module 12.

Optional Activity: Survival and Beyond: Strategies and Resources

Concept

Investigators consider the cumulative effect of racism on people of color, as well as on people who are white. Students see how racism impacts resources.

Sequence

In Module 12 investigators develop strategies that account for racism within their personal plans as they build support for themselves and others.

Instructions

You are interested in the impact of people hearing one another's experience in this arena, of sharing strategies that work. Some students will intuitively recognize approaches they have taken; naming them will be helpful. Others will hear new ideas and will recognize the importance of being intentional, especially when it comes to preparing children for life in North American society. The instructions below may be reproduced. A suggested facilitator narrative follows.

Survival and Beyond: Strategies and Resources

Let's look at the picture of "exploitation" again. We're going to talk about this in relation to race. We'll look more closely at this issue in order to begin the process of crafting personal strategies for dealing with racism in our daily lives. Recall the video "True Colors" (Sawyer, 1991) about Glen and John in Module 5. While there are regular experiences of inconvenience and frustrating hassles for all of us, for white people these are almost never related to race. They may be related to class, age, ability, gender, sexual orientation, etc., but not race. And they are not as predictable and consistent as the advantages related to race. (The experience of poverty is typically not the same for white people as it is for people of color. Race lays a subtle layer over the experience of poverty, which tends to moderate the experience and provide a different set of options.)

Discussion

1. Explore the cumulative effects of these everyday experiences on individuals—both **people of color** and **white people.**
2. **For people of color:** What are the cumulative effects of these daily inconveniences, hassles, embarrassments, and insults?
3. **For white people:** What are the cumulative effects of experiencing yourself, daily, as normative, racially speaking? How do the advantages that have been normalized impact the experience of being white?

4. **For people of color:** What personal, family, and community strategies (including church) work when it comes to the daily challenge of managing, negotiating, and handling these daily assaults upon your humanity? (Brainstorm some examples under each category—perhaps in small groups or, if the entire group is small in number, do it as a whole.)
5. **For white people:** What personal, family, and community strategies can you employ to "see" and "understand" these episodes that make racial consciousness the norm for people of color and socialize whites to be racially unconscious? What actions might you take when you "see" a situation that is advantaging you while putting a person of color at a disadvantage?

Note. From *Systemic Racism: Daily Strategies for Survival and Beyond,* by C. Valenzuela and J. Addington, 2006b, St. Paul, MN: Minnesota Collaborative Anti-Racism Initiative. Copyright 2006 by Minnesota Collaborative Anti-Racism Initiative.

III. D. Activity: Case Studies

Concept

This activity provides a chance to (1) practice scoring the extent to which resources do or do not exist and (2) practice "tight thinking"—being specific, clear, and analytical about one's assessment.

Instructions

To practice the scoring of resources, use the case studies from the workbook or case studies you create.

In this module we assess resources using two case studies. This tends to be a "safer" and less threatening way to introduce the concepts. In Module 9 the investigators will be doing their own self-assessment. Working on this is reminiscent of the typical agency assessment experience where people are more likely to be defined as "needy and deficient" and handed a treatment plan. Naturally, we want to avoid replicating that experience.

Keep students focused on objective information and point out subjective judgment calls vs. objective assessment. Some investigators are inclined to make sweeping (and oversimplified) appraisals of the case studies and their own resources. If that happens, work through the material again, using more precise questions to help students make accurate assessments of resources.

Focus on each resource the person in the case study has and the interlocking relationships of the resources. A severe problem in one resource may outweigh strengths in another. For example, a debilitating physical injury may overwhelm otherwise strong emotional resources or an educational advantage. Then focus on the strengths found in each resource, noting how strengths also can compensate for weaknesses. This pattern works both ways.

Sequence

The chart titled "Resources Scoring Table" introduces a rubric with five definitions for each resource, ranging from "Urgent/Crisis" to "Thriving/Giving Back." These are numbered 1 to 5 where 1 is low and 5 is high. In Module 9 these definitions and scoring mechanisms will appear again in an expanded format for self-assessment. Take a moment to go to Module 9 to see the expanded version of this table. You'll notice that for each box in this table there's a series of statements. You need not use the detailed scoring statements of Module 9 here in Module 7, but it's important that you know that we're introducing an idea and process here that will be reinforced later.

Remind the group of your timeline. How many sessions remain? This is important to note as the group begins to work toward closure.

III. G. Activity: College Services

Concept

Most students don't "recognize" the plethora of services available to them on campus. If they're from an under-resourced environment, they may never have used public libraries, museums, and other culturally oriented institutions. This investigation is intended to educate them about both what is available and why it's important.

Instructions

There may be opportunities to recognize and connect students to their interest areas, perhaps even interests they haven't yet discovered. Arts and literature events are entertaining and also a means of developing language skills, formal register, knowledge of hidden rules, and mental resources.

Some examples:

- Alumni organizations
- Arts (galleries, museums, theaters, movies, music, dance)
- Athletics (sports, recreation, wellness centers)
- Books (bookstore, textbook libraries, used-book buybacks)
- Career centers
- Car pooling
- Childcare
- Counseling centers
- Financial aid office
- Health clinics
- Registrar
- School catalogs and handbooks (large amounts of information, especially about policies)
- Student government
- Student organizations, including clubs
- Tutoring

Sequence

This continues the investigation of the campus community, fostering connectedness to place, peer relationships, and awareness of already existing resources.

MODULE 8

Stages of Change

Concept

It is important to recognize that change is an ongoing, fluid, and recursive process. It is rarely linear. Becoming aware of the process and articulating one's personal position within the process develops ownership or responsibility, as well as self-governance or control.

Learning Objectives: Investigators Will …

- Be introduced to and come to understand the stages of change
- Use the stages of change for building a future orientation
- Define motivation and being motivated
- Assess the stage of change inhabited by themselves and others in relation to going to college

Mental Models Labeled

None in this module.

Activities

I. A. Activity: Stages of Change for 'Going to College'

Concept

Students analyze their personal stories about their journey to college using the five stages of change as a framework. Other concepts, such as resources and hidden rules, also might be identified in stories. The goal is to help investigators gain power in their lives by taking charge of and monitoring their own changes.

Instructions

After asking students to think about how and why they decided to come to college—and what happened on the way—ask them to write down statements (on sticky notes) that describe the main events or elements at each stage. Also ask them to place the notes on the chart paper as they describe how they took the necessary steps to become a college student.

After all the investigators have placed their notes, facilitate the discussion about the collective experience of the group at each stage. Compare and contrast, looking for patterns and variations of the patterns.

Writing Assignments

Group Writing Assignment: Collective Biography

Introduction

Language shapes our identity and reality. We communicate and form relationships using language. We tell our story and hear the stories of others. Language plays a key role in tying our groups together. The assignment is to write a collective biography about the group.

Approach

Form groups of three or four people. Read this assignment together and talk about it. *Choose a name or identity for the group, so that you can talk about a collective "we."*

Determine who will be responsible for each section of the paper. You might want someone to take all the parts and do a final edit of the paper to tie it all together.

Decide how you will collect the information. You may wish to interview people separately or as a group. You could make up a questionnaire, do an online chat, or use e-mail.

The aim is to develop a group biography, not simply tell each person's story. You will need to collect the information, then sort and analyze it.

The areas of inquiry and questions provided in the next three columns are prompts. You may go beyond them or focus in on fewer of them, depending on what is most interesting about your group.

Roots

Where did you all come from? How many had parents who went to college? What kinds of work did everyone's parents do? What economic classes are represented in the group? How did people determine with which class they identified?

Education

What kinds of elementary and high schools did everyone go to? How many had parents who expected them to go to college? What advice did you get about going to college? Besides here, how many other colleges did people apply to? Who is the farthest from home? How many live in campus housing?

Work

What is the work experience of the group? How many people are working at what kinds of jobs? What kind of pay? How is the current economic situation affecting people and their work?

College Knowledge

What was it like being on campus the first two weeks? How did campus feel? What did the urban and rural students think of each other? What was it like dealing with various departments on campus? Did you have all the information you needed? If not, do you have it now? What worries you the most about being here?

Stress and Change

In times of stress, how do you keep yourself going? What do you say to yourself? What do you say when a friend is stressed? What do you do to stay motivated and keep going?

Future Story and Change

Why did the people in the group come to college? Besides an education and a good job, what else do they want out of life?

Language

Finally, be prepared to discuss in class how language was used to collect the information. Which register was used—and when? Which discourse pattern? What story structures? How did the group decide what to include or leave out? What do you as students personally think of the result? What did you learn about the other people in the group? What will other students be able to learn from your collective story?

Requirements

- Describes the experience of the group, not the stories of the individuals
- Is organized into well-developed paragraphs
- Is carefully edited and proofread
- Typed length: _____

MODULE 9

Self-Assessment of Resources

Concept

A clear and objective self-assessment is the foundation of the coming planning process where students will identify their resources—and how their strongest resources can be used to build other resources.

Sequence

Now the students consider their own experience, their concrete reality, in light of what has been investigated. The learning in the previous modules—"My Life Now," process of change, causes of poverty, hidden rules, resources, etc.—is all brought to bear on this personal assessment. The assessment then will be used as a basis for the upcoming personal plan for building resources.

This is another point in the sequence where investigators might express their motivation for change. It can be very personal and quite painful. One woman reported that she went to the restroom and wept for 20 minutes before returning with a determination to build her own resources and those of her children. At this point group members also might be supporting each other in various ways outside of class.

Learning Objectives: Investigators Will ...

- Come to understand and define their 11 personal resources
- Perform a self-assessment of personal resources
- Identify how knowledge of hidden rules can contribute to acquiring resources
- Begin considering strategies for building resources

Mental Model Labeled

- Personal Mental Model of Resources

Activities

I. A. Activity: Self-Assessment of Resources

Concept

As noted above, the concept for this activity is the same as for the module.

Instructions

It is suggested that you devote ample class time for students to complete the assessment and process the information. If assigned as "homework," it might not be done—and the investigators lose the benefit of the peer support that has likely developed.

The investigators know the importance of this module. Some people will be apprehensive about doing it, even dreading it. Your relationship with the investigators, along with their peer support, will be critical to the success of this exercise.

Remind the students that they have been doing solid, analytical thinking—tight thinking—during their investigations up to this point, and that is what they need to continue doing in the self-assessment. Remind them of the case studies they already assessed in Module 7.

The quality of the self-assessment will determine the quality of the plans, so it's important that people come to it prepared, having intentionally chosen an attitude of self-discovery and awareness of resources to support their persistence.

People in generational poverty are likely to have low resources. Some individuals in test groups went through the process, looked at their low scores, and began to revise them upward (note that the procedural steps address this inclination directly). Encourage investigators to resist the urge to "improve" their scores, focusing instead on intellectual detachment and objectivity, the same skills necessary to create realistic future plans.

Resources and Support

The sequence on systemic racism continues with the following questions to address issues of race as part of the personal assessment of resources.

Questions for people of color:

1. What support networks and resources are needed for you to thrive in the midst of the daily challenges posed by racism?
2. Do these networks and resources exist now? If not, how can you work with others to create them?

Questions for white people:

1. What do you need in order to maintain and deepen your awareness of the subtle ways race matters in your life?
2. What resources might assist you in thinking through ways you can be an ally to people of color as a white person who daily accesses advantage and support from the systems of society?

Note. From *Systemic Racism: Daily Strategies for Survival and Beyond,* by C. Valenzuela and J. Addington, 2006b, St. Paul, MN: Minnesota Collaborative Anti-Racism Initiative. Copyright 2006 by Minnesota Collaborative Anti-Racism Initiative.

Sequence

As described above, this activity draws upon all the preceding information. It now forms the foundation for the remainder of the course. In Module 10, students will consider what the community can offer them and also what they might contribute to the community (as an individual or as part of a group). The assessment of resources points to what resources might be considered priorities, which will focus the discussion in Module 11 on building resources. Finally, the assessment will inform investigators' Personal Plan for Building Resources—both with respect to which resources to target and which resources might support the development of others.

MODULE 10

Community Assessment

Concept

A communitywide perspective of the conditions and assets contributing to the quality of life is important because resources are built on a local level. While considerable data are readily available about standard economic indicators, the data collected for a social health index—a quality-of-life indicator—may or may not be easily accessible. This module allows teams of investigators to assess specific community conditions that may be of some personal interest, then collaborate to build a mental model of the community's assets or resources. There is a shift in focus toward a future orientation based on capacity, capabilities, gifts, and interests. The information is personalized by establishing links between each investigator's gifts and capabilities and those of likely associations and institutions.

Sequence

Investigators return to the second theme of the workbook: the impact of poverty on the community. The idea that investigators might "take a seat at the planning table" to solve community problems is made more explicit. Investigators will likely recognize the value of the information and capabilities they possess in that it is information and skills that many middle-class people and community leaders might not have.

This module also offers some relief from the intensity of the personal resource assessment, while it simultaneously sparks ideas for building resources to be used in Modules 11 and 12.

Learning Objectives: Investigators Will ...

- Negotiate within middle-class institutions through the use of mediation skills
- Develop skills for building a future story, including plans for community stability
- Develop the confidence and self-assurance to express themselves in relation to the environment of economic class and the causes of poverty
- Perform an assessment of community resources
- Identify areas of interest for personal civic engagement

Mental Models Labeled

- Group Mental Model—Community Resources
- Group One-on-One Relationships Mental Model
- Personal One-on-One Relationships Mental Model

Activities

I. A. Activity: Community Assets Assessment

Concept

Objective data are used to assess the social health of the community as it relates to people in poverty and the ability to move out of poverty.

Instructions

This assessment process might be suitable for a major project assignment if the course is offered for graded credit. It is conducive to group or team work.

You are encouraged to investigate conditions specific to your community or precipitated by national policies and events (such as the U.S. financial crisis of 2008 and 2009), in addition to what is offered here.

Sources of information to complete the assessment are highly variable and lend themselves to discussion of sources, credibility, objectivity, bias, etc.

Guide investigators toward making use of the expertise on campus to discover sources of data on the larger community. For example, faculty in health professions, education, and business may have excellent local sources of data. Workforce development departments and urban studies centers have specialized information toward which to guide investigators.

City, county, and state departments related to assessment areas generally post data on the Internet.

Investigators may want to invite community advocates and leaders to meet with their teams—or meet with the entire class—to help them assess how well the community is dealing with poverty and prosperity issues, or to present the groups' final mental models and report(s) to these leaders. This is another way to put learning and planning into the hands of the investigators so that it becomes *their* action. It's helpful if these meetings occur after some initial investigative work has been completed, as most agency and institutional personnel will tend to highlight their accomplishments and minimize their shortcomings.

A goal is to identify people from middle class for potential partnerships. Another goal is to assist investigators who want to become involved get to the decision-making tables in the community. These meetings between investigators and community members should be seen as the beginning of a relationship, not just an opportunity for one meeting with community leaders. It might be helpful to have students brainstorm (even rehearse with one another) how to open the interview, how to introduce the investigation, what information they wish to reveal about themselves or the course, and what questions to ask. Students can then give each other feedback about what worked well and what didn't work so well.

Then after the meetings with folks from the community and campus, debrief the experience in the context of what they've learned in *Investigations*—and discuss possible "next steps" that would foster and develop the relationships.

Some investigators might be interested in becoming more involved on campus and/or in community issues. For example, they may choose to advocate for improved housing, better-paying jobs, and fair credit opportunities. Or they might wish to become trained facilitators for *Getting Ahead* or *Investigations*. They may choose to partner with middle-class people on issues like land use and school issues. They might be interested in helping expand the use of *Investigations* on campus—or support incoming first-year students by serving as peer mentors.

Optional: The idea of sustainability introduced in Module 4 can be enhanced in the module if there is time. Interesting mental models on the subject can be found at *www.sustainablemeasures.com.*

Sequence

In this module we reinforce the work done in Module 2 (where we examined wages and housing conditions) and Module 4 (where we investigated the causes of poverty). The information gathered will support Module 11, which will investigate where to go in the community to build resources. We must not put the onus for action on people in poverty alone. Involving community members in the process of investigation provides an opportunity to debrief using the hidden rules as an analytical tool.

II. A. Activity: Creating a One-on-One Relationships Mental Model

Concept

Often the environment of poverty disconnects people in the community from the very associations and institutions most interested in and/or able to help them build resources. This exercise opens up possibilities not only by discovering what investigators can obtain—but also what they might *contribute.* **The idea of mutually beneficial or symbiotic capabilities, knowledge, and gifts can be transformative for students. There's a range of possible "seats at the planning table" that are discovered, which may be exciting for students inclined toward community engagement. That community may be the campus, the larger community, or both.**

Instructions

Encourage brainstorming; discourage "reality checks." This is an opportunity to shift the focus to future stories, to new visions, and to the beginnings of plans to get there.

To prompt and guide the discussion at this time, use the knowledge you have accumulated over time about the individual assets, talents, interests, and capabilities of the investigators.

Students may well identify numerous potential one-on-one relationships between themselves and individuals/resources in the campus community. For example: How is the campus going to support the investigators after they complete the course? What infrastructure exists that might form a natural confluence of capabilities and goals? Give some thought to this: Where are there potential champions with whom they might start? How might you support those connections?

Sequence

All the abstract information again becomes synthesized into concrete (potential) plans, illustrating both the process and stages of change from Modules 3 and 8, along with the hidden rules and resources addressed in Modules 5, 6, and 7. The building of this kind of human and social capital relates to the causes of poverty from Module 4. Some of the information discovered when considering gifts and capabilities of mutual interest might lead to modifying and revising the personal resource assessment findings of Module 9.

MODULE 11
Building Resources

Concept

The goal is not to develop "compliant students" but rather to develop those who are knowledgeable, focused, informed, self-directed, and eager to move on their own plans. Brainstorming opens up possible approaches, and the investigators get new ideas from one another. It's crucial to avoid "feeding" students with information and resources—to avoid leading them toward what they "should" do. Encourage creative, practical, and critical forms of thinking.

Sequence

Investigators connect the pieces of the sequence in new ways that are designed to develop their thinking about how to build resources, gain stability, and achieve goals. They can apply the process of change to describe their stage of motivation, intention, and willingness to act.

Learning Objectives: Investigators Will ...

- Be introduced to and come to understand processes for developing plans
- Identify opportunities to negotiate within middle-class institutions through the use of mediation skills and knowledge of hidden rules to build relationships of mutual respect
- Develop a future orientation by moving from concrete to abstract thinking in order to develop specific plans for personal growth
- Develop elements of their own plans for personal growth

Mental Models Labeled

None in this module.

Activities

I. A. Activity: Building Resources

- Option 1: Group Tic-Tac-Toe
- Option 2: Brainstorming

Concept

Everyone's story and everyone's self-assessment of resources will be different. These activities provide a way to help each other think of ways to build all 11 resources.

Instructions

There are two options for these brainstorming activities. The tic-tac-toe method will produce more possible solutions than simple brainstorming, but it takes longer. The tic-tac-toe directions seem complex and offer an opportunity to reinforce reading skills and procedural steps. You might use the opportunity to model how to follow procedural steps as you reproduce the tic-tac-toe chart.

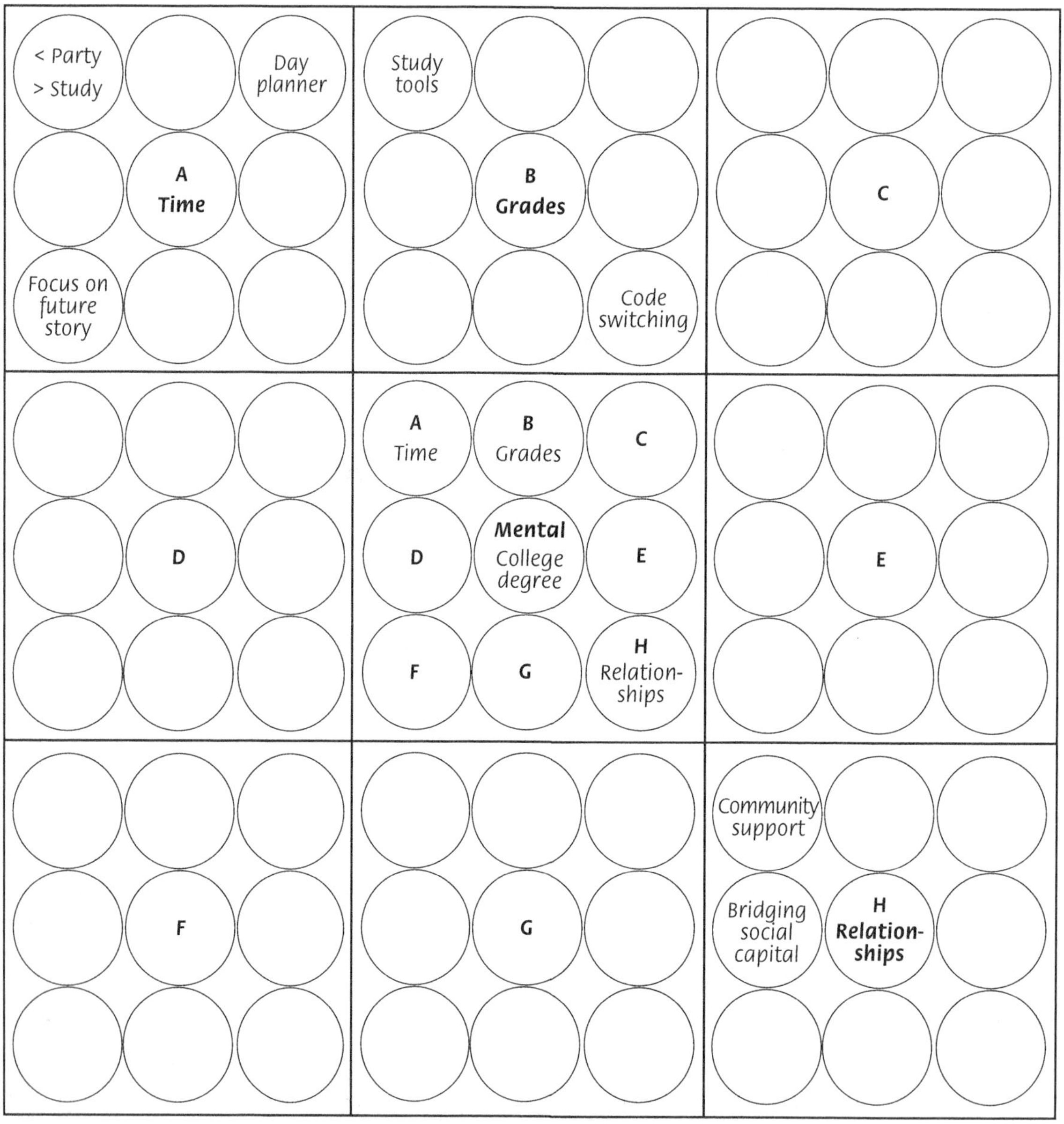

Start with the premise that, in the next module, investigators will be using stronger resources to build up weaker resources, whereas in this module it will become even clearer which resources are their strongest ones.

Introduce the idea of transition, reinforced with intention and motivation: *You can either stay where you are, doing what you normally do, or you can make a transition. That might involve beginning, continuing, or even clarifying a move toward whatever it is you want. With the tools discussed in this module, you can define the steps needed to get from where you are now to where you want to be in the future. Whatever the setting, you also can help each other make the transition.*

Treat this module like any other; it's an investigation. Do not have local agencies come in to tell the group about their services and programs—*unless* the investigators generate that idea themselves and there's general agreement in the group to do so. When investigators discover where and how to raise resources, it will be more powerful than sitting through agency or institutional "dog and pony shows."

The names of many agencies that appeared earlier when we were talking about the righting reflex and "Whose plan is it?"—as well as those identified in the community assessment and the college activities—will appear again. There may be mixed feelings about this because of past experiences with the agencies, but this is the opportunity to *reframe* the relationship between the investigators and the agencies. The shift in motivation and power makes all the difference. Imagine an investigator going to an agency (or student services department on campus) as a result of his or her *own* assessment—with the determination and a plan to build a particular resource. The motivation and power would now lie with the investigator.

This is when a partnership between middle-class agency personnel and campus student services on the one hand and the investigators on the other hand can be fostered.

Resources: Resources come from three places: communities, families, and individual actions.

- Strong, healthy communities can deliver well-paying jobs, good healthcare, good schools—and fair credit can help families build the resources of their children.
- Healthy, motivated families can pass on more than financial wealth to their children; they can pass on emotional, spiritual, social, and mental assets too.
- Individuals can choose to build their own resources and the quality of their lives.

Sometimes it's as simple as going to a bookstore and getting into the nonfiction section. Contemporary books are available on how to build every one of the 11 resources.

Hidden rules and cultural competence: It's in this exercise that it becomes quite apparent that using hidden rules is a choice. This choice was described as code switching in Module 6. Investigators will discuss the relative value of which rules to use. Middle-class rules sometimes will not be the only or best choice.

Further, this is when hidden rules can be used to resolve conflicts and improve outcomes. Most people fall into one of four categories in their understanding and use of hidden rules. The following four-quadrant chart might be a helpful concept to share as students explore when and where to use various rules.

Cultural Competence and Economic Class

	Unaware **of Hidden Rules**	***Aware*** **of Hidden Rules**
Incompetent **Using Hidden Rules**	Not aware of or intentional in the use of hidden rules. This applies to the vast majority of people.	Has learned about hidden rules but cannot or will not use them to build relationships of mutual respect. Uses hidden rules to exploit people from another economic class.
Competent **Using Hidden Rules**	People who have been raised in diverse, open, and loving environments can come to know hidden rules of other classes without knowing about Payne's Framework.	People who have learned about the hidden rules and use them to build relationships of mutual respect.

Closing This Module: Refer Back to the Planning Sequence

In addition to simply planning ahead to complete the work remaining, the group needs to begin thinking about overall closure. Remind group members how many sessions are left and estimate together the amount of work that lies ahead. This also continues the work toward closure. Follow the steps for the Backwards Planning exercise in Module 4 in order to prepare a timeline through the last class meeting, inclusive of all assignments and projects due.

I. C. Activity: Read a Good Book

Concept

These novels, biographies, and autobiographies about people from various economic classes encourage reading for pleasure. As an optional writing assignment, investigators can analyze the text using the theories of economic class, along with their personal experiences. (Discussion questions in the module can alternately serve as prompts for a writing assignment in lieu of in-class discussion.)

MODULE 12

Personal Plan for Building Resources

Concept

This plan constitutes one of the major goals of this effort, but overemphasizing it may backfire. It's better to provide class time to work on the individual plans as part of a low-key celebration, something that people want to join in. By working together and supporting each other, students will review and connect to all their past learning and work. In addition, they will project into the future, past the end of the course itself. The mental model of their future story can enhance the written plan by bringing out additional details and by creating an image, a vision to hold in the mind. Also involved in this final module is a group process of creating a plan for action on the campus and/or in the community.

Sequence

This is the culmination of the course where the investigators review all past work and consider its relevance to their future. It also sequences to what happens after the group ends—the longer term plan. Keep working toward closure, reminding investigators that the group sessions are almost over. Ask if there's anything special they would like to do at the last class session.

Learning Objectives

Through development of a personal plan, investigators will demonstrate understanding of:

- The causes of poverty
- The hidden rules of economic class
- Eleven resources
- Process of change

They also will:

- Demonstrate the ability to move from concrete to abstract thinking, thus improving the ability to solve problems and make changes
- Demonstrate application of the hidden rules to build relationships of mutual respect
- Analyze the strength of proposed plans based on the concepts of SMART goals and building resources
- Develop plans for personal growth
- Develop a sense of the value of and appreciation for abstract thinking
- Gain the confidence and self-assurance to express themselves in relation to the mindsets of economic class and the causes of poverty
- Develop a willingness to enhance their bridging social capital

Mental Models Labeled

- Personal Support for Change Mental Model
- Personal Mental Model of Future Story
- Mental Model for Community Prosperity and the College Campus

Activities

I. A. Activity: Personal Plan for Building Resources

Concept

Synthesizing the abstract information explored to date into concrete plans and action steps completes the process of change underlying the sequence. While there's more to come in terms of community engagements and closure, the personal plan is the capstone event.

Instructions

Blank worksheets for the seven-step SMART plans are in the workbook and the appendixes of the *Facilitator Notes.*

As we know, living on the lower rungs of the economic ladder tends to force people into a reactive way of solving problems, so don't assume that investigators have experience in planning or working through procedural steps. Please adhere all the way through to the steps in the workbook. Follow all the steps for each plan; students will probably identify two or more resources they want to build.

If facilitators can provide snacks, that will help create a mood of celebration. Ask the class what can be done to make this activity fun—and not feel like homework, a test, or as something imposed by somebody else. Don't stress the "individual" nature of the plan. That could seem too much like a test. Present it as something the group will do. Encourage students to talk and share while working on their plans.

We urge you to devote several hours (3–4) of class time to work through these activities as a group and communicate and support each other. This works better than assigning the activities as homework. (If investigators don't complete this activity, and it's perceived as homework, they're less likely to come to the next session.)

Investigators will create support teams to help them over the long term. Any assistance the campus and community can provide should be identified. The more concrete the ties between the investigator and various members of the team and community the better.

Building Resources: Consider intent and process.

- Motives: "What do I want?"
- Goals: "What will it look like when I've gotten there?"
- Task demands: "What do I need to get there?"
- Context: "What resources do I have to use? What constraints must I contend with?"
- Abilities: "What am I capable of doing?"
- Strategies: "Well, then. How do I go about it?"

Note. From "Enhancing Learning Skills: The Role of Metacognition," by J. B. Biggs, 1986. In J. A. Bowden, Ed., *Student Learning: Research into Practice,* 1986, Melbourne, Australia: University of Melbourne Press. Copyright 1986 by University of Melbourne.

Optional Activity: Pulling It All Together

Concept

For investigators of color, race will continue to create disadvantages in their lives that must be accounted for, and investigators who are white will continue to experience subtle advantages. Making this explicit helps all investigators come up with conscious intentional strategies that account for race.

Instructions

Discuss the following information and use it to revise the plans made to date. A suggested narrative follows.

Pulling It All Together

We have seen—and have done some work on—the importance of being intentional about strategies that help us survive, thrive, and provide support for one another in the face of the daily challenges of systemic racism. Clearly, we cannot understand the advantages experienced by people with white racial identity and the disadvantages experienced by people of color solely as expressions of personal prejudice and bigotry. They are the result of built-in biases; they are systemic. They result from white identity being normalized in this society. There is a tendency to frame our public conversations about racism only in terms of individual race prejudice and personal bigotry. Consequently, our society has not recognized and claimed responsibility for the subtle—and not-so-subtle—advantages that are automatically conferred (to white people) based on race. This built-in advantage for white society affects relationships in ways we normally don't see or talk about.

Discussion:

1. For white people: In the midst of dealing with poverty, are there ways that I can use the subtle advantages of white identity to help my family, my friends of color, and my community?
2. For people of color: Are there ways that I can counter the internalized messages from exploitation based on racial identity?

Sequence

This final activity recaptures and reinforces earlier learning and relates it to personal plans from the perspective of relationships.

Note. From *Systemic Racism: Daily Strategies for Survival and Beyond,* by C. Valenzuela and J. Addington, 2006b, St. Paul, MN: Minnesota Collaborative Anti-Racism Initiative. Copyright 2006 by Minnesota Collaborative Anti-Racism Initiative.

I. B. Activity: Personal Mental Model of Future Story (and) I. D. Activity: Mental Model for Community Prosperity and the College Campus

Concept

Students create mental models for their own future stories and for future community prosperity. Throughout the course, stability and prosperity have indicated more than financial wealth. Personal improvement can be achieved through self-awareness and self-direction. Resources can be built even while financial resources remain low. Here students envision a new future of their own and for their community.

Some learners are more visual than others, and you may wish to incorporate the development of the individual mental model with the development of the personal plan. Recall the concept of rolling revisions as the students add information and detail to the written plan, then the mental model, and vice versa. The closure and celebration continue as investigators work collaboratively, offering support and ideas for each other's personal vision, then practicing communication and negotiation to create a shared vision of the community's future.

Instructions

Challenge investigators to build on each other's ideas, to squeeze in more and more meaning, to represent all aspects of their plans.

Stop the group action from time to time to have people report in order to spur new thinking.

Discuss the mental model for Community Prosperity or for the College Campus. What would it take to realize this vision? Who would have to be involved? How long would it take?

Test the mental models against these criteria. A good mental model will:

- Include all important elements
- Identify time frames or timelines that show the past, present, and future
- Show the distinctions between individual and community responsibility
- Show the relative importance of the different parts
- Show the relationships between and among people
- Identify the key players
- Show options and possible consequences

These final mental models are products of the group that can be of value to outside community members.

Sequence

This brings together the two themes of *Investigations:* the personal examination of the investigator's life, as well as a personal vision of students' involvement with the broader community.

Writing Assignments

Future Story

Your final paper will consist of a narrative describing your future story,

Think about what you want your life to be like in five years. For example:

- Who are you?
- What will you have accomplished? How will your resource assessment look different from your original? How are resources connected to developing your future story?
- What do you do?
- What will you be doing? Work, school, family?
- What are the sights, sounds, smells?
- With what group do you identify?
- What will have changed in your personal life? Who will be around you?
- Where are you?
- Describe your living situation, the neighborhood; what are the sights, sounds, smells? What will be happening in your neighborhood or community? Will you be involved in any activities other than work and/or school? Will you be working to solve community problems in some way? If so, how?

- How did the changes in your life happen?
- Where will you be? How did you get there? What was the process?

Write your future story, incorporating some or all of the information above, as well as any other details you envision. Be specific.

Final Draft Requirements

- Is organized into well-developed paragraphs
- Is carefully edited and proofread
- Typed length: _____

V. Planning and Managing the Course—Before, During, and After

Course Design: the Purpose, Structure, Patterns, and Processes of *Investigations into Economic Class in America*

Purpose: *Investigations* provides a means of understanding oneself, individuals, and society through the lens of economic class. It develops cognitive skills and other resources that enable students to experience college success and envision a new future story. *Investigations* provides the missing link, enabling students to transfer their life experience to the college campus, and it provides a "Rosetta stone," teaching students to translate, at times literally, based on the needs of the setting.

Structure: Causes of poverty, hidden rules of economic class, resources for a stable life, and an intentional process of change support personal growth and engagements in the learning process. Applications can be within the campus, the larger community, and/or within social, political, and economic structures.

Patterns: *Investigations* uses mental models, mediated learning experiences, a distinct lexicon, and assessment/planning processes to discover new information and understand its relevance—and how it might be utilized to achieve and maintain change.

Processes: As an intentional sequence it begins by using the students' strengths in "situated learning"—telling personal stories and solving emergent problems and dilemmas. Through a process of co-investigations and assessments, students learn to utilize the framework of economic class, as well as to analyze and support their reasoning with new information and meaning. By directly teaching assessment and planning skills, problem solving becomes informed, proactive, and differentiated. Students learn to define and predict problems—and to seek the relationships and support necessary to address them. The group process of co-investigations, assessments, discussion/debate, and reflection build peer support and language skills. Creation of mental models develops abstract thinking and analysis, concrete planning, and future stories.

Scheduling and Pace

Three hours a week for 15 weeks is sufficient to cover the materials. Schedule no more than two sessions per week—but preferably one so you can work for a sufficient length of time each meeting.

As soon as the investigators grasp the material, move ahead, but encourage them to finish reading the text, to read additional sources, or to do an exercise on their own.

Make-up sessions and missed classes: The first time you use the workbook you may need to schedule make-up sessions for absences to ensure you begin each session with everyone at the same place in the content. This can be especially challenging at the start of the semester, depending on the institution's late admissions and add/drop policies. Early in the semester you may want to build in quick reviews at the start of each class. As your program develops, you might be able to assign the catch-up sessions to your co-facilitators, who have been drawn from previous semesters.

Suggested schedule of modules: Some modules will take longer than others, and you aren't held to this schedule. It's only a suggestion. Several sessions at the end make it possible for investigators to write up their plan, then review the course materials to make additional connections, enabling them to revise and refine their plans. Here is a suggested schedule.

WEEK	MODULE
Week 1	Module 1 Module 2
Week 2	Module 1, brief review Module 2, continued Module 3
Week 3	Module 3, brief review Module 4
Week 4	Module 4, continued
Week 5	Module 4, completed Module 5

WEEK	MODULE
Week 6	Module 5, continued Module 6
Week 7	Module 6
Week 8	Module 7
Week 9	Module 8
Week 10	Module 9
Week 11	Module 9 Module 10
Week 12	Module 10, continued Module 11
Week 13	Module 11, continued
Week 14	Module 11, continued Module 12
Week 15	Review all modules Conclude Module 12
Celebration	This can be part of the 15th session—or it can be a special gathering

Recruiting

Investigations is designed with first-generation, low-income, first-year students in mind, whether of traditional or non-traditional ages. Face-to-face contact with faculty and staff—and, preferably, past participants—is far more effective than mailings, handouts, and cold calls.

Using institutional processes:

Admissions office: Institutions have various terminologies for students admitted "conditionally" because of a weak academic history. Some of these students might be good candidates for the course.

Financial aid: Another means of identifying students would be in partnership with the financial aid office—looking for students with Pell grants, which are income-based.

Placement testing: Given the impact poverty has on students' language resources, placement test scores are one way to identify likely recruits. If the students' reading comprehension and writing scores are pre-college level, *Investigations* will probably be helpful academically.

Academic advisement: If students are required to meet with academic advisers, then this is theoretically an efficient means for recruiting/enrolling students.

Word of mouth: Graduates from the *Investigations* course might be your biggest advocates on campus until the program has proven itself in the eyes of the administration. If possible, pay students to help you with the recruitment process during orientation sessions and other events that bring first-year students to campus.

Community referrals: Various community agencies—Workforce Investment Act agencies, human services departments, women's shelters, veterans' services, etc.—can serve as a pipeline of students looking to build resources through education.

Stipends and Incentives

Some colleges continue the traditional model developed around the community-based Getting Ahead programs—that of providing stipends for participation. Such payments conflict with the middle-class mindset that says you shouldn't have to be paid to learn something that is going to better your life. Case in point: Middle-class students and their families pay for college, not the other way around. The security of a middle-class income allows people to know that today's needs are met so they can afford to focus on the future and the abstract.

On the other hand, people who live in poverty are living in the concrete and in the moment. The problems the investigators face require immediate action, and when a person is overwhelmed by the need to *act,* he or she likely won't be willing or able to learn. Thus a $15–$25 grocery or gas card each week solves an immediate problem. Once a relationship is established, students may attend partly because of the relationship, because they like the instructor. When the value of the information is realized, however, that may become the greatest incentive. If used, stipends are to be framed as payment for something that must be done, something beyond attendance. The work the investigators do—developing a Mental Model of Poverty, assessments of the community, and mental models for prosperity for themselves and the community—results in products. This output underscores the value of the knowledge students bring to the table and their ability as problem solvers.

Other incentives in keeping with the spirit of the course can symbolize many things. Hershey "Hugs" and "Kisses" symbolize development of social capital, while "Payday" and "$100,000" candy bars represent the longer term rewards to come. Academic calendars, three-ring binders, and loose-leaf papers support the organization and planning necessary for college success. Creative facilitators give each student a packet of Kleenex, a rose, and a dollar bill at the first meeting. These things symbolize the tears to be shed on the journey ahead, the beauty each person brings to the table, and the economic stability to be achieved through the process.

After the Course: Developing a Comprehensive Approach to Transition for *Investigations* Students

What do students do upon completing *Investigations*?

Some students grab the plans they made and pursue them directly, right through to earning their degrees. Along the way they build social capital, stabilize their environments, adjust relationships, and build resources.

Some students focus on stabilizing their environment or building particular resources, such as physical (health issues and recovery from addictions, for example), emotional (dealing with domestic violence and family crises, as well as building emotional management skills), financial (dealing with savings, Individual Development Accounts, housing, creditors, and predators), and spiritual. For this they need support from the typical governmental, non-governmental, and faith-based organizations for housing, transportation, childcare, and safety.

Some students focus on getting and keeping jobs. A well-paying job is a way out of poverty. The proven methods of a business like Cascade Engineering, along with such workforce development partnerships as Cincinnati Works, The Source, and Working Bridges, support graduates as they move toward self-sufficient wages by engaging local businesses and civic leaders. The core idea here is to create an employee assistance program that supports low-wage workers as they make the transition to well-paying jobs. Descriptions of successful programs that use Bridges principles can be found at *www.bridgesoutofpoverty.com.*

Some students focus on starting a business. Owning your own business is a way out of poverty. The community can establish or engage supportive structures for people who want to build a business, such as micro-enterprise initiatives and IDAs (Individual Development Accounts).

Some students focus on removing institutional, community, and systemic barriers. Bridges Steering Committees and Guiding Coalitions (described later in this section) must make it their work to knock down the barriers that people in poverty encounter. They learn what those barriers are by listening to investigators who are in transition out of poverty.

All students deserve support from the campus and community to stay in college and earn their degrees. Whether or not they get that support depends on how intentional the campus and/or community has been about building the necessary supports, be they academic or social.

Ongoing Support Beyond the *Investigations* Course on Campus

Evaluations and outcome studies indicate that investigators who have completed the processes described in *Investigations* are changing their mindsets and significantly increasing resources. How is the college prepared to support students after they complete the *Investigations* course? You will likely find it useful to consider how departments and services on campus—or partnerships with the community—can provide ongoing support. There might be natural places and spaces for the students to make the transition into as individuals and as groups. The Student Life or Student Services division/department is one of the most likely places to find programs and outlets.

Peer support: Students generally recognize the value of their new peer support and the need to develop additional bridging social capital to further their plans. Groups often want to continue to meet after the class concludes; they ask for *"Investigations II."* Course completers might want to form their own student organization, given the unique experience they have shared, and the likelihood that they have identified some common issues on campus or in the community that they would like to pursue. The student services sector of the institution is probably where guidelines about the establishment of student groups can be found. Perhaps you, the facilitator, would consider serving as an adviser to the group.

Support for engagement on campus: Some students become motivated to work on projects in the community or on the college campus. *Investigations* has equipped them with many of the tools they need to sit at the table and participate in the planning and evaluation of programs designed to meet the needs of people (including students) from poverty. The college campus is a living, vibrant, learning laboratory well-positioned to support and develop civic engagement strategies that capitalize on the strengths and skills of the *Investigations* graduates. In turn, course completers bring an energy and honesty to planning and evaluation committees that have the potential to motivate transformational change in institutional policies and procedures. Federal work/study and non-subsidized student employment funding can be used (for example) to hire graduates to:

- Recruit for the coming semester
- Serve as peer mentors to incoming first-year students
- Conduct surveys to document the results of their coursework and other efforts
- Serve on committees to analyze the Student Life Cycle (Becker et al., 2009)
- Work to educate staff and implement changes to the processes underlying the Student Life Cycle
- Participate in the planning and delivery of professional development for faculty and staff
- Represent college students on community committees

Academic strategies: *Investigations* is a powerful core for learning community models. When partnered with developmental or college-level writing courses and other gatekeeper courses, students build peer support and recognize the interconnectedness and relevance of their coursework. A second-semester learning community might include a service learning course. Through service learning, students can continue to use concepts related to economic class to better understand and reflect on a wide variety of service experiences. Practically every subject or service learning experience offers such opportunities.

Bridging social capital: The Circles™ Campaign from Move the Mountain is based on the premise that having bridging social capital is a way out of poverty. **By bringing people together across class lines, Circles builds connections that can be helpful to *Investigations* graduates, no matter which resources they choose to build. A Circles initiative can help students who want to stabilize their lives, work on health issues, pursue an education, get and keep a job, reenter society from prison, or start a business.** In this model, once the student completes *Investigations* he or she becomes a Circle leader. A coordinator matches the Circle leader to "allies" from middle class with particular skills or interests of value to the Circle leader and his or her plans for prosperity. The role of the allies is to guide, coach, and advise the Circle leaders as they work though their personal plans. Some colleges are partnering with Circles Campaigns in the larger community; some are considering adaptation of the model to the college campus. More information about the Circles Campaign can be found at *www.movethemountain.org* and *www.gettingaheadnetwork.com/college.*

Engaging the Campus and/or Community

Agency and organizational support:

The groundwork done in the community prior to conducting a group will influence the experience and success of investigators after the course—during the action phase. Community agencies that share an understanding of poverty, as well as the philosophy expressed in the introduction to this book, will be more likely to offer consistent approaches and support for investigators. Remember, the goal of this workbook is to help people develop specific goals for enhancing resources. Picture the investigators going to a community agency with their own plans in hand, motivated to utilize the resources offered by that agency. How that agency responds to someone motivated in that way can make a big difference to the person's future.

Community engagement:

There's a growing number of communities in the U.S. and Canada that are approaching poverty in comprehensive ways using the language and concepts presented in *Investigations.* This self-organizing is catalyzed in different ways. Often it's a result of educating a critical mass of educational or social service professionals about economic class and strategies for teaching or delivering services. These communities often develop Bridges Steering Committees (DeVol, 2010). People from all sectors (business, criminal justice, education, social services, civic, and faith-based) self-organize to provide cradle-to-grave strategies to address all causes of poverty and help people get out of poverty.

Such communities seek to provide *Getting Ahead* groups for people from poverty (*Getting Ahead* [*GA*] is the community-based version of the *Investigations* workbook). *GA* and *Investigations* graduates serve on Bridges Steering Committees, and some are employed at agencies making up the committee. In many cases, communities are implementing the Circles initiative as well.

If college representatives join a Bridges Steering Committee, they will find themselves in a community of practice that operates above the departmental level (above the "silos") where there's a shared intention to create communities where everyone can live well. Bridges Steering Committees create pathways out of poverty for individuals and redesign institutional systems and processes to better support them. Besides Circles initiatives, which provide middle-class allies, some communities offer IDAs, while others have connections to employers and provide support during the first year of employment. Some address the barriers that interfere with the transition from poverty to prosperity (DeVol, 2010).

There are opportunities for higher education to partner through Bridges Steering Committees. Initial work might focus on developing roles for *Investigations* graduates to play on the committee—or on building stronger links with social services to support the students' personal plans for prosperity. The spectrum of entities on Bridges committees offers opportunities to enhance student services, develop service learning programs, cultivate internships and apprenticeships, provide targeted education and training programs, and work on economic development strategies.

Supporting institutional change:

> The challenge of integrating what is known about adult learning theory, economic class, and effective teaching practices is considerable. There is a need to make higher education more learning-centered so that the educational experience increases in value and promotes a more genuine learner agency that [fosters] autonomy, engagement, and mastery. (Becker et al., 2009, p. 165)

***Investigations* provides a foundation on which to build. Students who complete the course can be a source of significant energy, creative ideas, and honest feedback for program designers and front-line staff. As more faculty members become educated about economic class in relation to their field of expertise, they will increasingly incorporate these ideas into coursework. Student services staff will think about these ideas in relation to the campus and use the information about hidden rules to analyze internal processes.** Both faculty and staff will utilize the Student Life Cycle as they consider ways of increasing student access and success without lowering expectations.

Please visit *www.gettingaheadnetwork.com/college* and share your program descriptions and developments. We want to hear from you.

Appendixes

Appendix A

Investigations into Economic Class in America

Purpose of Each Module

Prepared by Philip DeVol, with Kathy McPherson, Lenore Moore, and Tammy Schoonover

Every module in *Investigations* has two purposes:

1. **The purpose of the content knowledge of each module.** This knowledge base about poverty is generated by the investigators themselves as they share their insights into the impact that poverty has on them and their community. They also contribute to the knowledge base by identifying barriers to transition on campus and in the community. Further, the investigators explore the new information found in each module.

2. **The purpose of the learning process that unfolds module by module.** The sequence and reinforcement of the learning experience are intentional. They offer an opportunity for members of the group to learn the change process, articulate their own motivation for change, and build a plan for their own future story.

In the following table, the Content Knowledge can be shared with the investigators, while the Process Purpose is for the facilitator to know.

Module	Content Knowledge	Process Purpose
1. Introduction	Explain how the group will work. Establish "ground rules" for governing the group. Establish a comfortable thinking environment.	Interest the potential participant in joining the group. Establish the role of the facilitator as someone who is not superior to the group but someone whom the group can work with in a co-investigative and synergistic way.
2. Mental Model of Poverty	Describe what poverty is like in the community. Identify individual resources: debt-to-income ratio, percentage of income for housing, wage realities. Define what each person's life is like right now.	Establish that the investigators have valuable information that others need to know: what poverty is like. Establish what life is like now so that investigators can decide if they want to make changes as the class moves through the modules. Encourage investigators to see the strengths in their own story and to become powerful.
3. A Process for Change	Investigate how to make changes by thinking in the abstract, even during a chaotic situation ("the tyranny of the moment"). Look/reflect on life experiences from the outside in (from the abstract to the concrete) rather than the inside out (from the concrete to the abstract). Move from "I can't because …" to "I can because …"	This concept can help free people from the tyranny of the moment. Only some people will get this idea right away, but if the facilitator reinforces this learning as examples come up during discussions, the entire group will get it by the end. Many goal plans in social services require clients to establish goals/objectives while they're actively in the concrete—while they're often immobilized and unable to see anything outside their immediate situation. This type of planning rarely achieves success; clients may sign the plan out of obligation, resignation, or compliance rather than motivation.

Module	Content Knowledge	Process Purpose
4. Rich/Poor Gap	Discover that poverty is caused by more than one thing; there are many causes that must be addressed by people at all levels. Establish Mental Models of Middle Class and Wealth.	Connect the concrete experiences of poverty to seemingly abstract information—e.g., connecting low wages to how globalization works or how the lack of manufacturing jobs in the community makes it hard for people to get out of poverty. Establish the difference between a stable economic situation (middle class) and a powerful and very stable situation (wealth) and an unstable situation (poverty), reinforcing the mental models created in Module 2.
5. Hidden Rules	Discover the rules investigators are currently accessing. Learn the rules of the middle class so that people can navigate the world of work and school more skillfully. Learn the rules in order to develop relationships of mutual respect with others.	Empower people to understand and navigate the middle-class institutions, as well as to build relationships and social capital.
6. Language Rules and Resources	Learn how to use language differently and more fully, according to the situation. Discover ways to think about language—registers of language, discourse patterns, story patterns, and voices in order to be more skillful at code switching, mediation, and negotiating.	Address directly one of the barriers that many under-resourced students face at college. Introduce ideas on how investigators can use the information to improve relationships, resolve conflicts, and write Standard American English. Like other topics introduced in *Investigations,* some follow-up on the part of the investigators may be necessary to deepen the grasp of the material.

Module	Content Knowledge	Process Purpose
7. Eleven Resources	Define poverty as the degree to which a person has the 11 resources. It's not just about money, it's about a high-quality, balanced life. Discover the domino effect of resources; investigate how one issue leads to another—for better or worse.	This definition gives people in poverty and communities something to do about poverty: build resources. Case studies prepare investigators to think about their own resources and lead to the self-assessment in Module 9.
8. Stages of Change	Describe how change takes place so everyone can be aware of and intentional about his or her own process.	Encourage people to be in charge of their own change process. The workbook itself assists investigators through the stages of change from old mindsets to new mindsets.
9. Self-Assessment	Each investigator establishes his or her individual resources—both high and low.	Resources were introduced in Modules 6 and 7. Now the students will do an assessment that can show them which resources they need to build. They will also learn what their strongest resources are and how to use high resources to build low resources.
10. Community Assessment	Establish the strengths and weaknesses of the community. Identify individuals, associations, and organizations that can help build resources. Identify the gifts and abilities of individuals who are valuable to those organizations. Share results of the investigation with the campus and community.	Poverty isn't just about the mindset or actions of the poor, it's also about what is available in the community. Discover assets on the campus and in the community that can contribute to building resources. Engage investigators as problem solvers on campus and in the community.
11. Building Resources	Learn how to build resources.	This is a natural outcome of the work done in previous modules; it prepares investigators for the final module.

Module	Content Knowledge	Process Purpose
12. Your Plan	Develop an individual plan based on informed choices. Review SMART goals—define, identify, and practice. Create a one-page mental model that represents the journey from "My Life Now" to "My Future Story." Create a mental model for how the campus and/or community can support transition and help people attain economic stability.	Put old tools and new tools to work. Ideas and concepts are now being put into action. This is an end product, but it's really the beginning of new relationships with the facilitator and other group members. The hardest work of *Investigations* is to provide long-term support for students. Facilitators, administrators, community leaders, and the investigators themselves can all play a role in developing the necessary structures.
Closing and Transition	This is an opportunity for the investigators and facilitator to celebrate the work that's been done and to express appreciation for and to one another. Many groups have celebrations, make certificates, and conduct follow-up meetings as they make the transition to the activities described in "What do students do upon completing *Investigations*?" (see section V. in *Facilitator Notes*).	This work is based on the understanding that people in poverty are problem solvers. Many investigators want to help others and to help their communities. Former investigators can join those who plan and run *Investigations* on campus, *Getting Ahead* in the community, and Bridges Steering Committees. The information that investigators have about the realities of poverty (created in mental models) and the barriers that people face as they build economic stability is foundational information for community planners. *Getting Ahead* is being done in more than 100 sites. Bridges communities, campuses, and organizations that provide *Getting Ahead* are urged to engage the community so that investigators get the support they need. Bring closure to the investigators' work and recognize that relationships are entering a new phase.

Appendix B

Sequence and Reinforcement of Key Concepts

found in

Investigations into Economic Class in America

Purpose: The purpose of Appendix B is to help facilitators become aware of the learning sequences embedded in *Investigations into Economic Class in America* and to encourage facilitators to use them to deepen the learning experience for the student investigators.

Audience: "Sequence and Reinforcement of Key Concepts" is for facilitators who are already familiar with *Investigations.* It is assumed that the facilitator has read the Overview and Sections I–III in *Facilitator Notes,* as well as the book *Understanding and Engaging Under-Resourced College Students* (Becker et al., 2009). Facilitators are encouraged to familiarize themselves with resources found on the *Getting Ahead* website, including the information found in the "college" tab: *www.gettingaheadnetwork.com/college.*

Importance of sequencing and reinforcement: When facilitators sequence and reinforce information through activities, discussions, and the use of mental models, it will not be necessary to "teach" or to "hit a home run" with any concept the first time it appears in the workbook. People who have completed *Getting Ahead in a Just-Gettin'-By World* (the community version of *Investigations*) have referred to the learning process as layered, something that goes deeper the farther you progress.

Sequence: Knowing the sequence of certain ideas, the facilitator can consciously attend to covering the content at each encounter. There is no need to "telegraph" the sequences to the investigators. It's better for the facilitator to set the process in motion but allow the learners to discover the connections for themselves.

Reinforcement: Linking the learning to previous content need not be formalized either, but instead let it evolve as a natural outgrowth of the investigations. The collection of mental models that hang on the walls in the order of their development can be used by the group to label and record new thoughts on former ideas.

The importance of dialog: Experience tells us that investigators learn as much or more from the dialog that arises from the activities as from the activities themselves. The activities are designed to spark reflection and discussions. Getting through every exercise or activity in a module isn't as important as providing time for discussions.

Format: There are five sequences described here. Several other sequences are explained earlier in *Facilitator Notes*. The first two sequences below are described module by module because they unfold over several modules. The remaining three, while just as important, are described briefly. When facilitators weave the sequences together skillfully, the learning experiences become more powerful. These sequences will work naturally when the investigators can discuss their insights thoroughly.

SEQUENCE 1: Income and Wealth Disparity and the Hidden Rules of Class		
Explanation: In short, income and wealth disparity leads to distinct differences in the way people experience life in the United States. These environments (Mental Models of Poverty, Middle Class, and Wealth) give rise to the hidden rules of each class. Knowledge of the hidden rules helps people develop relationships of mutual respect and resolve conflicts. These understandings also help investigators build resources and participate fully in planning and decision-making boards.		
Module	**Content: Mental Models and Activities**	**Meaning (Explaining the Links) and Tips**
2	Mental Model of Poverty	The very first mental model defines what poverty is like locally. It establishes the idea of class environments. ***Tip:*** Label it accurately. Following group discussion, put the analytical terms, such as *instability, concrete, relationships, tyranny of the moment,* and *problem solving,* around the Mental Model of Poverty.
4	Investigate Income and Wealth Disparity Create Mental Models of Middle Class and Wealth	Where there is extreme disparity in income and wealth in a nation, there will be sharp differences in the way people experience life in that country. These two mental models, plus the one on poverty created in Module 2, make up the three environments of class. ***Tip:*** Compare and contrast the three environments and put key analytical terms on the mental models.

Module	Content: Mental Models and Activities	Meaning (Explaining the Links) and Tips
5	Hidden Rules of Class	The hidden rules of class evolve out of the environments of class (the three mental models), which in turn derive from income and wealth disparity. ***Tip:*** Listen to the stories told by investigators from the very first day to pick up examples of hidden rules that are used and broken on campus. These can be used to illustrate the hidden rules.
7	Definition of Poverty Mental Model of Social Capital	The many causes of poverty and the instability it generates make it difficult to maintain resources or to build them. The mental model of Social Capital establishes the degree to which an individual has bonding and bridging capital. This sequence opens a space for investigators to see the value of relationships with individuals from all economic classes, to find the people with whom they have relationships of mutual respect, and to see the possibility of establishing new relationships using their new learning. ***Tip:*** Let the *group* make the connection between the hidden rules and the development of bridging social capital: Be an *observer* to the learning taking place in the group.
9	Self-Assessment of Resources	Knowledge of hidden rules can now be seen as a valuable skill. The shift from judgments that break relationships to understandings that form relationships brings with it a degree of power and influence. The hidden rules can help investigators navigate the societal systems they encounter and build resources ***Tip:*** There need not be much discussion during and after the self-assessment. While this can be very painful, let the group provide support to its members. Encourage the group to look to the planning phase that will follow.

Module	Content: Mental Models and Activities	Meaning (Explaining the Links) and Tips
10	Community Assessment	Doing a community assessment is in keeping with the "two story" pattern in the workbook: the individual's story and the community's story. Poverty isn't just caused by individual choice and behavior but also by what exists in the community. This reinforces the learning that occurred when developing the mental models of class, the causes of poverty, and the importance of social capital. While the assessments of community agencies tend to be negative, the investigators may find individuals inside those agencies whom they trust. Identifying key individuals (from diverse backgrounds) reinforces the concept of bridging social capital introduced in Module 7. ***Tip:*** Taking a thorough look at the community for strengths and weaknesses can reinforce the importance of community as a source for change and resources, as well as a place that needs to make changes that benefit people of all classes.
11	Build Resources and the Support for Change Mental Model in Module 12	The last step in building a plan of action is to create a mental model that identifies the people investigators want on their support team. This can include people from the group itself, friends and family, and those with whom they have bridging social capital. ***Tip:*** Observe how many of the investigators have used this sequence to create relationships across class lines to address poverty on campus and in their own community.

SEQUENCE 2: Process of Change, Building a Future Story

Explanation: Learning and using the process of change has the potential to free a person from the tyranny of the moment. This happens to civilian populations in war, victims of natural disasters, people in persistent poverty, and individuals in economic and medical emergencies.

The process of change gives people the power to think about their own thinking, also known as metacognition. Individuals can become aware of a focus that is narrowed to the now, to the concrete problem that stares them in the face, and allows them to think in the abstract, to reflect on the future, and to make plans that will free them from the control of the now.

The process of change for *Investigations* is introduced early in the workbook so that investigators have enough time to encounter the idea again in later discussions. It is made explicit in Module 3, but the sequence actually begins in Module 2.

Module	Content: Mental Models and Activities	Meaning (Explaining the Links) and Tips
2	Mental Model of Poverty "My Life Now"	The analysis and labels that are written on the mental models developed in Module 2 will feed the development of the process of change. Group discussion and analysis of the Mental Model of Poverty may generate these terms: *concrete, unstable, relationships, problem solving,* and *tyranny of the moment.* ***Tip:*** The facilitator can introduce the terms when the concepts are being expressed. They can be added to the lexicon of terms that will be developed throughout the workbook.
3	Mental Model of Process of Change	The facilitator will draw the mental model on chart paper. That mental model must appear on the wall with all other mental models. The terms developed in Module 2 will be necessary to sequence the ideas. ***Tip:*** Take the time to explain "planning backwards" and procedural steps found at the bottom of the Process of Change mental model.

Module	Content: Mental Models and Activities	Meaning (Explaining the Links) and Tips
4	Predators	Predators take advantage of people (especially those in poverty) because of these three things that are covered in the process of change. Predators provide concrete solutions for *concrete* problems and they tend to do it quickly. Predators form *relationships* of understanding and respect (often sham), for example: "I'm here to help you. I understand your need for (fill in the blank) right away." Predators rely on the tyranny of the moment, knowing that if they do the first two effectively, it is very unlikely that the customer will analyze the situation, the contract, or the fine print. ***Tip:*** This is a time when people can apply that process of change in very concrete ways. They can stop using the services of the predators.
8	Stages of Change	People in poverty are busy solving problems; stopping to analyze the situation (as is done in *Investigations*) is difficult to do, so one stays in Pre-Contemplation. Moving through the stages of change presupposes that life is fairly stable. Relapse and failure to maintain the change can be linked to instability and the tyranny of the moment. Knowing this process of change can help someone complete his or her goals. Knowing the stages of change can put people in charge of their changes. ***Tip:*** Facilitators cannot force someone to be motivated or to change. Facilitators can only support people as they move through the stages of change. Investigators will progress in their own way and on their schedule. The facilitator cannot expect to "herd" a group of investigators through the process together at the same time.
12	Your Plan	Planning backwards, as taught in Module 3, will help people see the value of that tool and the importance of creating procedural steps. Knowledge and use of the process of change can keep investigators focused on their future story in the midst of chaos; it is the stabilizing factor.

SEQUENCE 3: Relationships During Transition

Going to college means giving up some relationships for a period of time and building relationships with people from different backgrounds. This can be harder for people from poverty than for people from economically stable situations. This phenomenon is not often discussed, but it can play a big role in whether or not a student stays in college and completes a degree.

The idea that pursuing achievement can complicate relationships is named explicitly in Module 5, but the sequence begins in Module 2 when the group makes the Mental Model of Poverty and talks about how important relationships are to survival. "Your people" also comes up when naming the people who sleep in your house. Every time friends and family are mentioned, this sequence is being addressed. It isn't necessary for the facilitator to make the point or name the sequence; the group discussions will go in that direction … or they won't. The issue comes up again when building a mental model of Social Capital in Module 11 and when making the Support for Change mental model in Module 12. By then, the facilitator can be certain that the group will have talked in depth about relationships and achievement.

SEQUENCE 4: Motivation

It can be safely assumed that students taking the *Investigations* course are motivated to attend college, but it can't be taken for granted that they are motivated to investigate or take action on economic class issues or necessarily to make good use of their time in this course. Fortunately, *Investigations* is designed for those who tend not to be motivated, as well as those who are.

The facilitator's job is to help students explore all that there is in this course about economic class and to trust that most of the students will discover their own motivation sometime during the 12 modules. There is no sequence for this, even though change is addressed directly throughout the course, particularly in Modules 3 (process of change) and 8 (stages of change).

Experience shows that there are certain points when investigators begin to express motivation for change. They are:

- **Module 2:** Directly after determining the debt-to-income ratio or the percentage of income spent on housing. Many people determine right then that they must do something differently, and some begin making changes immediately.
- **Module 4:** When investigators look into the debt they have accrued because of predatory lenders, some begin to make concrete steps. It takes a long time to get out of debt, but the desire to change is often first articulated then.
- **Module 7:** When learning that poverty is about the lack of resources, some people begin to talk about building resources. Doing the mental model of Social Capital is another point when people start making their own argument for change. They begin to see that they can take steps to form relationships of mutual respect with people on campus and in the agencies.
- **Module 9:** Many investigators will express their desire to change when they create the bar chart of personal resources after doing the self-assessment, if they haven't done so before.

Tip: When it comes to making the argument for change, it should be the voice of the investigator you hear, not your own. The role of the facilitator does not include connecting the dots for an investigator or pointing out what resource needs to be built first. The other group members might do that in the course of the discussions; they might challenge one another or even confront each other. But the facilitator, who represents the dominant culture (and who has special status), should resist the urge to tell investigators what to do.

Having issued that caution, it's important to say that there is real joy in hearing investigators express their motivation and take charge of their lives. Facilitators of Getting Ahead say this tends to be the best reward for facilitating the process.

SEQUENCE 5: Relationships with Other Members of the Group, Campus, and Community

Relationships within the group: Experience shows that the well-established group development process (forming, storming, norming, and performing) usually manifests itself in *Investigations* as well, but with added intensity. Module 2 is challenging as the investigators face in very concrete terms the impact that poverty has had on them personally. The relevance of the early modules brings the group members together quickly. The layering of information and the deepening of the dialog also serve to tighten the bonds of the group. It's common for group members to help each other through a crisis in daily life, to assist each other in study groups, and to share information on how to manage campus life. Group members often continue to meet informally, and sometimes formally, with or without the support of the sponsoring organization.

Tip: This process is so ingrained in group work that it doesn't require action on the facilitator's part. The group will form in ways to support each other, or it won't. It is theirs to own.

Relationships with the campus and community organizations: Under-resourced students whose families may have been involved with service providers and the other community institutions are likely to view those organizations with distrust. The college is generally perceived the same way. In Module 2, when students are building the Mental Model of Poverty, many stories will be told illustrating how that distrust was "earned." Again, in Module 4, when exploring the causes of poverty in the community and learning how predators work, the sense of anger and distrust can be expected to arise. In Module 4 the group also will likely deepen its understanding of middle class and wealth by creating mental models of those environments.

In Modules 5 and 6 students will learn about hidden rules and language issues and how that information plays out in community life. When investigators learn and talk about the hidden rules of the campus life (from the financial aid office to social life), it smooths the rough edges of the class divide and fosters the sense of belonging. In Module 7 the investigators will create a mental model of their own social capital. It's during that exercise that there is sometimes a shift in mindset about organizations. Now, instead of distrusting the entire organization, it is about trusting particular people inside those organizations—people who might be bridging social capital. Later, in Module 10, the group will assess the resource-building capacity of the organizations and determine which organizations, or individuals within them, are worthy of consideration.

Tip: In the early modules when investigators criticize campus or community organizations, don't defend them or offer explanations. It's more important that you listen, that you learn the realities of the investigators, than it is to correct what you think are inaccurate statements. In later modules, when evaluating social capital and organizations, it's fair to require the objectivity and factual information that may have been missing in the first few sessions.

All of the *Investigations* work is based on relationships of mutual respect. Attending to how the group functions together—how relationships are developed on campus and in the community—is directly tied to staying in college and completing a degree. It's also tied to finding the organizations and individuals in the community to partner with in order to locate work, build resources, and build a balanced life.

Appendix C

Responding to Student Writing

[Portions of the following section are adapted from *Understanding and Engaging Under-Resourced College Students* (2009), by K. A. Becker, K. M. Krodel, and B. H. Tucker. Highlands, TX: aha! Process.]

As the facilitator, you will have to decide whether to use writing assignments and, if used, how much weight they carry in terms of grading, if indeed the students will receive a grade. Writing is used here to help students translate, figuratively, their oral discussions and thinking into more formalized written communication, and to develop their thoughts and elicit certain responses. **The goal is not to focus on grammar and mechanical issues, but rather elicit and shape the complex stories and wisdom students bring to the classroom but have not yet found ways to talk about.**

Certain modules have suggestions for writing assignments, which are included in the *Facilitator Notes*. You are free to use all, some, none, or replace them with your own. The assignments that appear in the *Facilitator Notes* seek to accomplish several things:

- An early assignment asks the student to tell their story and the work history of their family. This serves to illuminate aspects of their primary bonding relationships and will help them keep their connection to home even as it evolves. The last assignment develops the students' personal future story, inclusive of family and community.
- There are assignments that ask students to identify with an economic class and explore the issue of belonging to a group. A later assignment involves developing a group biography. This takes the concept of group even farther and promotes development of positive peer relationships.
- The large amount of content in Module 4 lends itself to a research paper/term paper assignment, if that would be appropriate for the class. Such an assignment offers multiple opportunities to practice with the learning strategies described in Appendix D.
- Code switching (see next page) is employed to demonstrate the legitimacy of non-standard primary discourse, as well as the impact of personal choice on one's ability to communicate and be understood.

- Mediation gets tied back to the concept of change through the analysis of "Transformational Mediation."

Regardless of the weight given to writing assignments, we offer here three practical strategies for responding to student writing intended to develop cognitive skills, self-exploration, and expression—and avoid stifling creativity.

Content/process focus: Ignore mechanical errors. It is vital to refrain from editing—from pointing out punctuation, spelling, grammar, and usage errors—in order to focus fully on the act of writing rather than the mechanics. Mike Rose (1989), director of UCLA's Writing Program, and Mina Shaughnessy (1977) point out the futility of concentrating on grammatical mistakes. For the under-resourced student, as with many basic writers, "error is more than a mishap; it is a barrier that keeps him not only from writing something in formal English but from having something to write" (Shaughnessy, p. 11). Rose states:

> The assumption is that error can be eradicated by zeroing in on the particulars of language. And that assumption seems to rest on a further (erroneous) assumption that grammatical error signals some fundamental mental barrier to engaging in higher level cognitive pursuits: until error is isolated and cleared up, it will not be possible to read and write critically, study literature, or toy with style. (p. 141)

Linguists have proved three critical concepts:

- First, students who use "home language" (casual register with patterns that show possession, past tense, etc.) are not deficient in their thinking, they simply have not learned a secondary pattern of discourse.
- Second, linguists have demonstrated that "the red pen" absolutely does not work and might even exacerbate the use of one's home language.
- Finally, they have demonstrated at all grade levels that code switching is a proven tool for adding more formal or Standard American English to the students' language repertoire (Wheeler, 2008).

Students first must come to the realization that they have ideas to express—and that they are able to express them. Then grammar and syntax become relevant when the students want to share their ideas and their writings—and they realize that in order to be taken seriously in certain contexts, the paper also needs to be grammatically and syntactically sound in relation to the patterns in Standard American English.

Use labeling: Just as students are developing a lexicon for economic class and change theory, so too does this technique facilitate a shared understanding of the kinds of writing found in student journals and assignments and how they might improve it.

An example:

A writing sample begins: "Are you a person with plans and dreams of your own? Do you reach for the stars? If so, then the *Investigations* personal planning process is for you!"

The facilitator asks, "How does this sound? Does it remind you of anything? Where have we heard this sort of talk before? How would you label it?"

The student might respond saying, "This sounds like one of those Ronco commercials late at night on TV." Following a discussion of Ronco commercials (to ensure that all students are familiar with the concept), this then would be labeled "the Ronco voice" for the rest of the term. When the facilitator writes "Ronco" in the margin, the student automatically understands exactly what is meant.

By establishing this kind of shared lexicon through class discussions, it's far more likely that students will grasp the meaning of the "Ronco" label on their paragraph rather than a lengthy, abstract explanation. You can have a student maintain and update the list for the rest of the class.

Other examples of labeling marginalia might be:

"By working hard and doing the right thing, my family made it out of poverty."	Magic dust
"Being a student means different things to different people."	Golly gee whiz-ism
"Try hard to succeed at what you want out of life."	"Be good" advice
"It was wrong for me to watch TV instead of study."	Bad guys/good guys

Labels for common rhetorical issues might include:

Conclusions that don't conclude but rather stop or dodge	"Pinning the tail on the donkey"
Introductions that don't introduce—or simply repeat from the assignment	"Warm-up pitches"

And here are some examples of marginalia that recognize good thinking or writing:

Connections between ideas, use of theory to support ideas, etc.	"A mind at work"
Insights, perhaps not yet clearly stated	"Diamonds" and "Diamonds in the rough"
Skillful analysis, solutions, and conclusions	"Bringing something to the table"

Questioning: Another type of marginalia for writing assignments is short but powerful questions, also useful in prompting class discussion. For example:

1. How so?
2. In what way?
3. Why, do you suppose? That is, how do you account for such a thing?
4. Meaning what, exactly? That is, what does one do when one … (works hard, is patient, uses his or her mind, reads, studies)?

The four questions above can become a litany or routine to the extent that students begin asking the questions of themselves prior to submitting the assignments. The questions naturally draw students to the real heart of the assignment and help them develop authentic ideas. Students think about their thinking and their writing.

Additional commentary questions for writing assignments and student conferences include (Craig Paulenich, personal communication, November 14, 2008):

1. How might it be argued that …
   a. You've neglected, underestimated, skipped _______?
   b. You've failed to do justice here to what you know?
2. How might it be argued that this text could have been written by someone who has never actually (for example) lived in poverty, raised a family, been a teacher, been a student, used a relationship to solve a problem?
3. If you could retain only one or two places in this text, where would it be?

Students are held accountable for their language and their text through questions that indicate the instructor is taking them seriously, that language matters. The purpose of these questioning and labeling techniques, as well as the focus on the content rather than the mechanics of student papers, is to create invitations that open up the text and their minds to new ways of imagining—and to better enable students to discover for themselves.

Appendix D

Strategies for Teaching Students How to Learn

Our thought processes and feelings manifest themselves along a continuum. At one extreme we are pure emotion—concrete and sensory-based. On the other end is pure intellect, detached, theoretical, and highly abstract. Neither extreme is particularly healthy or functional. Students who are overly emotional drop out of school when they get angry with someone at the school, while teachers show bias toward certain groups of student based on their emotional reactions to them. On the other end, the overly intellectual student has trouble building relationships or articulating the passion in, say, a piece of literature, while instructors analyze and dissect student performance, failing to respond to the students' personalities and needs for connection.

Students from low-resource environments often come to college needing more language skills (1) to express their emotions rather than act upon them, (2) to learn cognitive strategies to make increasingly complicated connections among pieces of information, and (3) to reason at higher levels of abstraction. (Meanwhile, as staff and faculty some of us would do well to detach intellectually a bit and consider whether or not the normalization of our academic world has impaired our perception of our own emotions and even our ability to adequately and accurately experience them.)

Emotional	Expressive	Intellectual	Analytical
Sensory feelings	Language/emotions	Mental models	Causal models
Impulsive	Representational systems	Abstract constructs	Systemic theories

As noted in the opening section on the Process of Teaching and Learning, this workbook places emphasis upon language development through vocabulary and reading. *Investigations* also can be used as the context for directly teaching sub-skills: the sorts of learning strategies useful for college students in this and other coursework—and even beyond.

Developing the Act of Thinking

Investigations offers opportunities to build skills in each of the three phases in the act of thinking identified by Howard Sharron and Martha Coulter (2004, p. 60).

Input Skills *affect the quality and quantity of data gathered*

1. *Highlighting, note taking, outlining:* Rather than highlighting, students with poor input skills "color" the entire page, not differentiating the key ideas from the rest of the text. It's also common to see students frantically trying to write down every word the facilitator says. You can demonstrate these study skills using *Investigations*—particularly Modules 4, 5, and 6, which are rich in content.
2. *Organizing space and time:* Modules 2 and 3 contain planning exercises that provide a window into the level of organization in the students' lives. You might be surprised how unaware students are about planning behaviors and keeping an organized notebook of assignments. You can model the importance of this skill by requiring students to have an academic planner or calendar and *bringing it to class each meeting.* Demonstrate its use at each meeting by looking ahead at due dates and planning backwards to accomplish goals. If maintenance of the planner is a course requirement and academic grade points are assigned, students will be more likely to approach the task seriously and transfer the newly acquired skills to other courses and life situations. Simple rewards like candy, pens, etc., reinforce the behavior and also can generate a bit of good-natured competition within the group.
3. *The abstract world of paper:* For concrete thinkers, the volume and significance of paperwork generated by our institutions are overwhelming. In Module 2 use the activity "Floor Plan" to highlight the importance of having a space to store registrations, financial aid, tax returns, grades, and past assignments.
4. *The even more abstract world of computers and the Internet:* Realize that issues with computer use go beyond mere knowledge of how to use the word processing program. Students with input issues will likely also have a great deal of trouble understanding *where* the information (document, spreadsheet, PowerPoint presentation) physically *is* on the computer and how best to organize and locate files. Realize that students might not find these skills relevant until a critical mass of confusion has developed. In other words, perhaps toward the midpoint of the term, students will be more interested and motivated to attend a workshop for this purpose. Demonstrate how to bookmark websites and do Internet searches.
5. *Organizing information from various sources:* Modules 4, 5, 6, and 7 lend themselves to additional activities and assignments requiring students to gather information from more than one source.

a. The tried-and-true method of recording bits of information onto 3x5 cards and then sorting the cards into categories still works.

b. Some students also need to sort their bits of data into "relevant" and "irrelevant" categories.

c. A "cause and effect" model also teaches students to sort, for example, the causes and the effects of poverty.

Elaboration Skills *affect how efficiently data are used*

1. *Comparisons:* Students will describe one item and then the next and the next, never referring to the other item. Module 5 offers excellent opportunities for building this skill, while also differentiating *comparison* from *judgment.*

2. *Hypothetical thinking:* Modules 2 and 4 ask students to create mental models of the environments of economic class, helping them learn to generate information from information provided and construct hypotheses. Similarly, the information about code switching in Module 6 lends itself to application of contrastive analysis and the scientific method (Wheeler, 2008).

3. *Projecting virtual relationships:* The discussions offered throughout the workbook provide opportunities to help students identify the logical evidence to support their definition of a problem or solutions, as well as logical reasons for their opinions. This is referred to as "tight thinking." Modules 3, 5, 6, 11, and 12 are especially useful.

4. *Strategies for hypothesis testing:* Students who become committed to their opinions or hypothesis before testing them will learn numerous ways to improve the complexity of their thinking through classroom discussions. Modules 6, 9 and 10 are especially helpful.

5. *Summative behavior:* Students who have difficulty measuring progress toward their goals will benefit from the insistence upon using the academic calendar, as well as the planning processes undertaken in Modules 4, 11, and 12, and measured against the process of change in Module 8.

Output Skills *affect the ability to communicate the outcomes of elaboration processes*

Oral and written communication: Impulsive and egocentric communicators, students who "block" or cannot express their thoughts, and those who have trouble following the logic paths toward answers all benefit from the design and sequential nature of *Investigations.* The heavy reliance on discussion, group interaction, and possible writing assignments provide opportunities to model and teach verbal and written communication.

Specific Strategies

Planning

Planning is a theme throughout the modules—on a small scale early on as students are asked to first define how they spend their time, attach meaning to their experience, and then construct a small plan for completing a midterm or final assignment. The planning sequence culminates in personal plans for prosperity and the community's future story. The more emphasis on and modeling of planning behaviors (use of calendars, "To Do" lists) the better.

Drilling down breaks large assignments into the component parts.

1. First have students write out in their own words their understanding of the assignment.
2. Review and clarify the students' understanding of the assignment.
3. Working backwards from the definition of the completed assignment, identify and list the large items that must be completed or actions that must occur to create the final product.
4. Sort the list into "levels"—in other words, sort the larger tasks from the detailed tasks.
5. Create a "drilldown" map (see next page).
    a. With the end goal to the left, draw a line and write in one of the larger tasks.
    b. From that larger task, draw lines and write in the sub-tasks that will result in the larger task being completed.
    c. If the sub-tasks need detailed tasks, draw them in as well; in other words, expand the numbers of steps and level of detail to increase clarity and specificity.
    d. Create a timeline and place the tasks along the timeline.
        i. Check the timeline for time allocated to proof, print, bind, or "finish" the project.
        ii. Check the timeline for "buffer" to account for emergencies.
        iii. Identify and highlight the intermediary milestones.
    e. Transfer the information to the academic calendar and daily "To Do" lists.
    f. Assign priority to "To Do" lists—A and B being most critical to the project's success or most time-sensitive.

'Drilldown' Plan for Going to College

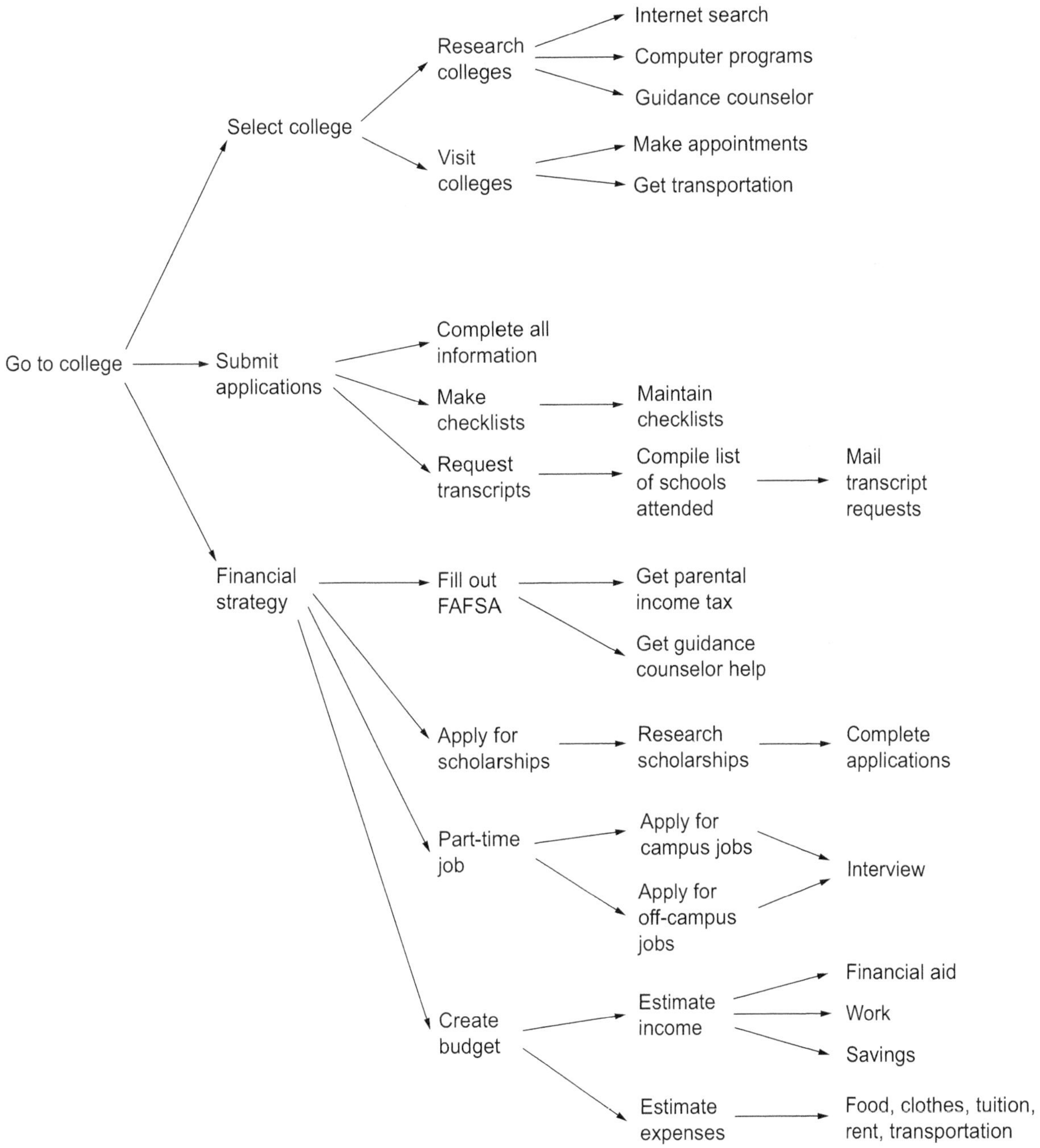

Semantic Maps for Vocabulary

In addition to the built-in lexicon in *Investigations* there are other ways to work with vocabulary. Module 6 emphasizes language and introduces terms with nuanced meanings. Semantic maps can help students understand the meaning of a work by examining: What is it?, What is it like?, and examples. This exercise can support students' efforts in creating mental models or illustrating the lexicon.

Penance/Forgiveness

What is it?	What's it like?	What are examples?
Reparation	Compensation	Reimbursement for pain and suffering
Apology	Making amends Atonement	Confession of wrongdoing Confession of sins Child or adult voice
Sacrament	Self-punishment	Wearing a hair shirt

Conflict

What is it?	What's it like?	What are examples?
Discord	Disagreement, argument, fracas, dispute, controversy	Arguing with your partner, child, or parent voice
Fight	Battle, skirmish	War, boxing

Resolution

What is it?	What's it like?	What are examples?
Solution Outcome Deal Settlement	The answer, the upshot	Contracts, treaties, adult voice

Negotiation

What is it?	What's it like?	What are examples?
Cooperation	Working together	Agreeing to focus on strengths and abilities
Compromise	Give and take	Finding middle ground, each side giving concessions
Integrative	Win-win	Finding middle ground, each side winning Adult voice

Concept Feature Analysis

This offers a way to examine the relationships among pieces of information. The Community Sustainability Grid in Module 4 is such an example. The CSG examines the relationships between and among the four areas of poverty research and five levels of activity under way (or not). Students can use the CSG to research and plan the strategies that could be used on a college campus to help students from low-income backgrounds. They could research best practices in recruitment, retention, education, and so on, then find who is responsible on your campus for such activities and research what they are doing and why. This is foundational work for later activity in Module 11 and beyond for campuses interested in engaging students in their institutional planning and evaluation committees.

Concept Maps for Organizing and Differentiating Information

Concept maps help to organize ideas, associate ideas, and make connections among them. When addressing the complex and interlocking concepts in Module 4 or Module 7, maps depict the elements and the connections among the elements.

1. Identify a central idea: The following two examples use the rise and decline of the middle class as the central idea.
2. Define *subordinate* ideas. Here they are represented by the four clusters of research into the causes of poverty (individual choices, community capital, exploitation, and political/economic structures).

Policies That Built the Middle Class

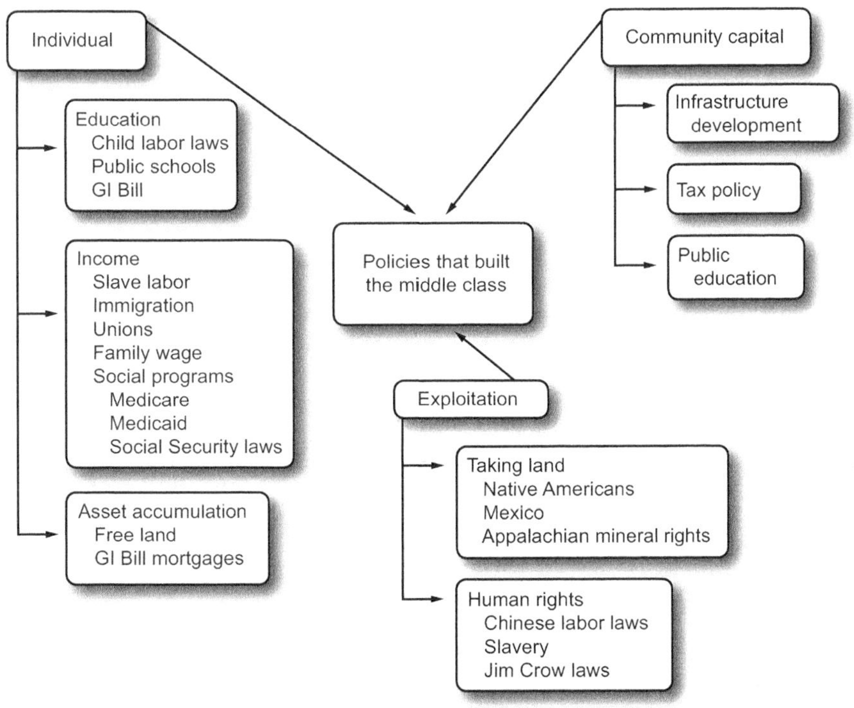

3. Identify more refined subordinate ideas to branch from there—for example, policies that affect individuals do so by affecting their ability to attain an education, increase their income, and accumulate assets.
4. Use and reinforce key words from the lexicon; this helps memory. You also may use colors, symbols, and mental models in the mind map.

Process Mapping

A process map is a graphic representation of a procedure, showing inputs, outputs, and start and end points. Process maps might include steps, people to be involved, time, and costs. The information in Modules 8–12, in which investigators consider the stages of change, how to build resources, and create plans, lends itself to process mapping.

These are a few specific techniques that may enhance the process of teaching and learning undertaken throughout the *Investigations* workbook. These learning strategies help students master content, understand its meaning, and learn how it relates to them. As always, please share successful strategies specific to this workbook or the needs of students at *www.gettingaheadnetwork.*

Policies Reducing the Middle Class

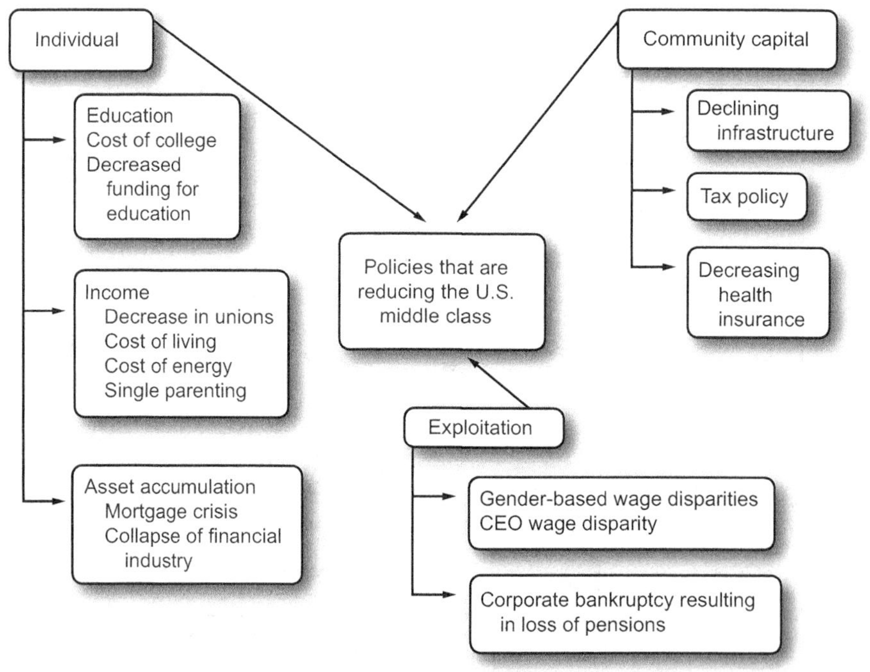

Appendix E

Adult Learning Theory Related to *Investigations* Process

Adult Learning Theory	Application in *Investigations*
The learner's most significant resource is his or her experience.	*Investigations* places value and meaning on the under-resourced students' experience with the effects of economic class on their community and their personal lives.
Learning occurs best through contextualized situations.	The contrast between life and the new situation on the college campus is used to illustrate concepts.
Learners value experience and discovery.	Students use their life experience to create questions for investigation—about how economic class affects a person and community. The richness of the subject matter allows for tangential exploration and extrapolation.
Relevance is important. Learners need to know the rationale for what they are being taught.	Examining one's life situation and experience is highly engaging, and doing so in the context of creating a successful stable life and/or succeeding in college is highly relevant. Actionable information addresses real barriers to campus engagement.
Education is a transactional process, with teacher and learner continually engaged in negotiating priorities, methods, and criteria of evaluation. Adult learners want to be more independent and self-directed, yet learners need to be guided toward independence and self-direction.	The process of co-investigation is a transactional process, and students work independently and in groups to investigate issues of personal interest and relevance. The facilitator acts as co-investigator, resource, and guide.
The heart of adult learning is critical reflection—self-examination and assessment of one's assumptions and beliefs, which leads to perspective transformation. Perspectives are sets of assumptions built over time, through which new experiences are filtered and understood.	*Investigations* provides a process for self-assessment of resources and analysis of one's driving forces and use of hidden rules leading to transformation of the students' assumptions and perspectives about economic class, their role as students, and their choices.
Through reflection, learners' perspectives become more inclusive and integrated. Perception distortions are (1) epistemic—internalized concepts as representing right/wrong, good/bad; (2) sociocultural—generalized beliefs about specific populations; and (3) psychic—assumptions that produce anxiety and block certain behaviors.	Students look critically at perspective distortions, such as racism, classism, their own generalizations and stereotypes compared with others', and how their personal perspectives influence their behaviors.
The process of learning and becoming educated is fundamentally different from vocational skill training.	*Investigations* is not vocational training, but it does teach additional patterns of language and behaviors the learner may choose to use based on the needs of the situation.

Note. Adapted from *Understanding and Engaging Under-Resourced College Students* (p. 185), by K. A. Becker et al., 2009, Highlands, TX: aha! Process. Copyright 2009 by aha! Process.

Appendix F

Sample Course Descriptions, Syllabus, and Lesson Planner

Three Sample Course Descriptions

- *Investigations into Economic Class in America* provides a means of understanding individuals and society through the lens of economic class. Information about hidden rules and resources develops success skills and enables students to understand and operate effectively with diverse populations in new situations.
- *Investigations into Economic Class in America* investigates the impact of economic class on individuals and communities. By examining society's rules and how to build resources, individuals can stabilize their economic environment and become active leaders in the community.
- *Investigations into Economic Class in America* applies a structured process of change to individual and societal issues of economic class. Students co-investigate what constitutes stability personally and in relation to the broader community. Assessment, analysis, and planning for change are key components of the course.

Sample Syllabus

Class Meetings: Monday/Wednesday, 12–1:15

Instructor:

Karla Krodel, BSN/MBA
E-mail address: kmkrodel@ysu.edu
Department of Social Work
3033 Cushwa Hall

Office hours: Tuesday and Thursday, 12–1, and by appointment
Office phone: (330) 941-2464
Office address: 1027 Jones Hall, YSU

Required Textbooks /Supplies:

- *Investigations into Economic Class in America,* DeVol & Krodel, 2010
- Additional handouts—provided
- Three-ring notebook, notebook paper
- Academic calendar

Course Objectives/Outcomes:

Knowledge Base—Students will be introduced to and come to understand:

1. Research into the causes of poverty
2. The hidden rules of economic class
3. Eleven resources for a stable, rich life
4. Process of change
5. Assessment processes
6. Planning processes

Skills—Students will:

1. Negotiate within middle-class institutions through the use of mediation skills
2. Develop skills for building a future orientation, including plans for personal growth
3. Use formal register to express self, tell stories, write, and negotiate
4. Develop the ability to move from concrete to abstract thinking, thus improving the ability to problem-solve and change
5. Identify the mindsets of other people in relation to the hidden rules of economic class

6. Develop skill in use of hidden rules to build social capital and relationships of mutual respect
7. Analyze the strength of proposed plans based on the concepts of building resources and SMART (specific, measurable, attainable, realistic, time-specific) goals
8. Develop plans for personal growth

Attitudes and Dispositions—Students will develop:

1. Intellectual detachment that enables informed choices
2. The confidence and self-assurance to express themselves in relation to the mindsets of economic class and the causes of poverty
3. A willingness to develop bridging social capital
4. Appreciation for diverse cultures and the effect of normalization on societal issues

Weekly Assignments and Topics

(More or less class time might be devoted to modules; assignment dates will stand)

Week	Topic	Readings—and Assignments Due
1 Jan 11, 13	Introduction: Getting Started— Understanding Poverty: "My Life Now"	Module 1–2
2 *Jan 18 off* Jan 20	Understanding Poverty: "My Life Now" Power: Process of Change	Module 2–3 Reflection Journal Mods 1–3 due W
3 Jan 25, *Jan 27, no class*	Understanding Poverty: The Rich/Poor Gap	Module 4
4 Feb 1, 3	Understanding Poverty: The Rich/Poor Gap	Module 4 Reflection Journal Mod 4 due W **Writing Assignment 1**
5 Feb 8, 10	Framework: Hidden Rules of Economic Class	Module 5
6 Feb 15, 17	Framework: Hidden Rules of Economic Class, Language, Code Switching	Module 6
7 Feb 22, 24	Framework: Language Resources, Negotiation	Module 6 Reflection Journal Mod 5 due W
8 Mar 1, 3	Framework: Eleven Resources *Portfolio check and midterm conferences*	Module 7 **Writing Assignment 2**

Week	Topic	Readings—and Assignments Due
Spring Break, Mar 8–12	*Spring Break*	
9 Mar 15, 17	Understanding Where I Am: Stages of Change	Module 8 Reflection Journal Mod 6 due W **Writing Assignment 3**
10 Mar 22, 24	Understanding Where I Am: Self-Assessment *Portfolio check and midterm conferences*	Module 9 Reflection Journal Mod 7 due W
11 Mar 29, 31	Understanding Where I Am: Community Assessment	Module 9 Module 10 Reflection Journal Mod 8 due W
12 Apr 5, 7	Power: Building Resources	Module 11 Reflection Journal Mod 9 due W **Writing Assignment 4 (Group Project)**
13 Apr 12, 14	Responsibility: Your Plan for Getting to Prosperity	Module 11 Module 12 Reflection Journal Mod 10 due W
14 Apr 19, 21	Responsibility: Your Plan for Getting to Prosperity	Module 12 Reflection Journal Mods 11–12 due W **First draft** of Personal Plan due W **First draft** of My Future Story due W
15 Apr 25, 27	Responsibility: Your Plan for Getting to Prosperity—the Community *Portfolio review*	Module 12 Review and revision Reflection Journal 13 due W
16 May 3	Finals Week Closing and Transition	**Portfolio** due on day of final **Final Writing Assignment/Plan**

ASSIGNMENTS

1. **Attendance/participation:** Your attendance and participation are crucial not only for your own learning but also for your classmates. Class expectations for accountability will be discussed in class. Each week is worth 25 points. There will be opportunity to make up missed classes outside of class time.
2. **Ten journal reflections:** Directions are attached.
3. **Four writing assignments, final assignments, and personal plan:** Specific writing assignments will be distributed during the course of the semester.
4. **In-class assignments:** In addition to discussions, there are other in-class investigations, particularly the creation of mental models, mini-plans, and assessments, which will be presented as part of your portfolio.
5. **Portfolio:** Your portfolio will consist of:
    a. Ten journal reflections
    b. Four writing assignments
    c. Activities from *Investigations* workbook (mental models and mini-plans)
    d. Final writing assignment: My Future Story
    e. My Personal Plan for Growth

    Items will be placed in the three-ring notebook in chronological order. The portfolio will be discussed individually in a conference with the instructor during the mid-point of the class and during the last week of class.

ASSIGNMENT GRADING POLICY

	Points
Attendance/participation	400
Ten journal reflections	100
First writing assignment	50
Second writing assignment	50
Third writing assignment	50
Fourth writing assignment (group)	50
Future story	100
Final personal plan	100
Portfolio	100
Total points from assignments	**1,000**

COURSE GRADING POLICY

Points		Letter Grade
900+	=	A
800–899	=	B
700–799	=	C
600–699	=	D
Less than 600	=	F

COURSE POLICIES

Revised Assignments: You may, and are encouraged to, revise any assignment as many times as you wish to improve your grade.

Late Assignments: Ten percent will be deducted from the grade for the written assignments for every class day the assignment is late. Journal assignments must be turned in the week they are due unless you have an excused absence.

Attendance: Class attendance is crucial. Each week is worth 25 points.

Punctuality and Classroom Etiquette: These are essential elements of success in this course. See Student Handbook regarding disruptive student behavior. Turn off cell phones and electronic devices.

Academic Conduct: Submitting work of other students as one's own—or plagiarism—results in penalties ranging from an "F" on an assignment to expulsion, depending on the seriousness of the offense.

Students with Disabilities: In accordance with the university policy, if the student has a documented disability and requires accommodations to obtain equal access in the course, please contact the instructor at the beginning of the semester or when given an assignment for which accommodations are required. Students with disabilities must verify eligibility for accommodations with the Office of Disability Services at (330) 941-1372 and/or TDD (telecommunications device for the deaf) at (330) 941-1564.

Outline of Content and Activities: ***Investigations into Economic Class in America***			Core material for in-class discussion	Suitable for small-group work	Suitable for out-of-class assignments	Adult student orientation
MODULE 1: GETTING STARTED						
I.	Introduction		X			
II.	Using *Investigations into Economic Class in America*		X			
MODULE 2: MENTAL MODEL OF POVERTY						
I.	Mental Models: Background		X			
	I. A.	Activity: Group Mental Model of Poverty	X			
II.	Housing					
	II. A.	Activity: Affordable Housing Payment Threshold Calculator	X			
	II. C.	Activity: Mental Model of the Floor Plan of My Apartment/House	X		X	
III.	Wages					
	III. A.	Activity: Getting Ahead or Just Getting By?	X			
IV.	Savings					
	IV. A.	Activity: What Is Your Savings Cushion?			X	X
V.	More Rules of Money					
	V. A.	Activity: Calculating Your Debt-to-Income Ratio	X		X	X
VI.	'My Life Now'		X (discuss in class; complete outside of class)		X	
	VI. A.	Activity: Personal Mental Model—'My Life Now' (Mental Model Pie Chart)				
VII.	Time Management and Planning					
	VII. A	Activity: Time Management (Where Does the Time Go?)			X	
Writing Assignment: Write Your Family History					X	
MODULE 3: A PROCESS FOR CHANGE						
I.	Who Wants You to Change?		X			
	I. A.	Activity: Examining Agency Approaches to Change	X			
II.	Change Meets the 'Righting Reflex'		X			
III.	College and the Process of Change			X	X	
	III. A.	Activity: Deciding to Change		X	X	
IV.	*Investigations'* Process of Change		X			
V.	Time Management: Becoming More Effective				X	
	V. A.	Activity: Becoming More Effective			X	

		Outline of Content and Activities: ***Investigations into Economic Class in America***	**Core material for in-class discussion**	**Suitable for small-group work**	**Suitable for out-of-class assignments**	**Adult student orientation**
MODULE 4: THE RICH/POOR GAP AND HOW IT WORKS						
		Optional Activity: Systemic Racism/'Handedness'	X			
I.		Research on Poverty				
	I. A.	Activity: Identifying and Detaching from Predators	X	X	X	X
II.		The Rich/Poor Gap: Economic Disparity				
	II. A.	Activity: Real Family Income Growth by Quintile and for Top 5%; 1946–79 and 1979–2006	X			
	II. C.	Activity: CEO Pay as a Multiple of Average Worker Pay; 1960–2007	X			
	II. E.	Activity: Ownership of Household Wealth in 2007—'The Ten Chairs: the Difference Between Wealth and Income'	X			
III.		The Intersection of Race and Economic Class	X			
IV.		Who Pays the Most Taxes? What Does It Mean to the Community?			X	
V.		Wealth and Access to Power: Disparity in Wealth as a Cause of Poverty			X	
VI.		More About Mental Models				
	VI. A.	Activity: Mental Models of Middle Class and Wealth	X	X		
VII.		Putting All These Ideas Together to Develop Sustainability	X			
VIII.		Utilizing the Four Areas of Research to Bring People from All Political Persuasions and Economic Classes to the Planning Tables			X	
IX.		Time Management and Planning: Setting a Goal and Working a Plan			X	
	IX. A.	Activity: Backwards Planning			X	
Writing Assignment: Economic Class					X	
Research Assignment: Issues and Causes					X	
MODULE 5: HIDDEN RULES OF ECONOMIC CLASS						
I.		Defining the Hidden Rules of Economic Class	X			
II.		Key Points to Provide Perspective on the Hidden Rules	X			
III.		Suggestions on How to Study the Hidden Rules	X			
	III. A.	Activity: Studying the Hidden Rules	X	X		
IV.		The Hidden Rule of Power				
	IV. A.	Activity: Power and Public Policy		X		
		Optional Activity: Exploring Everyday Racism—'True Colors' Video	X	X	X	

Outline of Content and Activities: *Investigations into Economic Class in America*			Core material for in-class discussion	Suitable for small-group work	Suitable for out-of-class assignments	Adult student orientation
MODULE 5: HIDDEN RULES OF ECONOMIC CLASS (continued)						
V.	Hidden Rules of College					
	V. A.	Activity: Hidden Rules in College		X	X	
	V. C.	Activity: Hidden Rules of Financial Aid		X	X	
	V. D.	Activity: Hidden Rules of Campus Social Life		X	X	
Writing Assignment: Essay About 'Differentness'					X	
MODULE 6: LANGUAGE RULES AND RESOURCES						
I.	Registers of Language		X			
II.	Discourse Patterns		X	X		
III.	Code Switching					
	III. A.	Activity: Code Switching in Personal Writing Samples			X	
IV.	'Voices': Parent, Child, Adult		X			
V.	Story Structure		X			
VI.	Vocabulary		X			
VII.	Mediation: the *What,* the *Why,* the *How*		X			
	VII. A.	Activity: Mediation in the College Classroom		X	X	X
	VII. C.	Activity: Getting Time to Study Through Mediation		X	X	
VIII.	Using Language to Resolve Differences		X			
IX.	Using the Language of Negotiation			X		
	IX. A.	Activity: Negotiating for Ugli Oranges			X	
	IX. F.	Activity: Self-Assessment of Negotiating Skills				
MODULE 7: ELEVEN RESOURCES						
I.	Defining Poverty		X			
II.	Defining Resources		X			
III.	Additional Information on Five Key Resources		X	X		
	III. A.	Activity: Mental Model of Personal Social Capital	X		X	
		Optional Activity: Survival and Beyond—Strategies and Resources			X	
	III. D.	Activity: Case Studies	X (discuss in class; complete outside of class)	X	X	
	III. G.	Activity: College Services			X	

Outline of Content and Activities: ***Investigations into Economic Class in America***			**Core material for in-class discussion**	**Suitable for small-group work**	**Suitable for out-of-class assignments**	**Adult student orientation**
MODULE 8: STAGES OF CHANGE						
I.	The Stages of Change		X			
	I. A.	Activity: Stages of Change for 'Going to College'		X	X	
Group Writing Assignment: Collective Biography				X	X	
MODULE 9: SELF-ASSESSMENT OF RESOURCES						
I.	Willing, Able, and Ready					
	I. A.	Activity: Self-Assessment of Resources	X (provide in-class time)		X	
MODULE 10: COMMUNITY ASSESSMENT						
I.	Assessing Your Community		X			
	I. A.	Activity: Community Assets Assessment		X	X	
II.	Asset-Based Community Development					
	II. A.	Activity: Creating a One-on-One Relationships Mental Model		X	X	
MODULE 11: BUILDING RESOURCES						
I.	Key Points About Building Resources		X			
	I. A.	Activity: Building Resources		X		
		Option 1: Tic-Tac-Toe Technique		X		
		Option 2: Brainstorming			X	
MODULE 12: PERSONAL PLAN FOR BUILDING RESOURCES						
I.	Building Resources		X			
	I. A.	Activity: Personal Plan for Building Resources	X (provide in-class time; encourage additional revision out of class)		X	
	I. B	Activity: Personal Mental Model of Future Story		X		
	I. D.	Activity: Mental Model for Community Prosperity and the College Campus		X	X	

Appendix G1

Sample Directions for Journal Reflections

As the syllabus notes, you must keep an ongoing journal, which includes your responses to the information discussed in class each week. You also may include mental models, drawings, ideas, and/or "To Do" lists. However, only the required journal responses will be graded and count as part of your final grade.

At the end of the semester, all journal responses will be submitted as part of your portfolio.

RESPONSE [Required length: approximately 300 words].

In your journal response you get to write about what you think or feel regarding the information being covered—or about some specific part of the module. Some modules have specific journal assignments, but most of the time you can take your journal response in whatever direction you wish. You might:

a. Give your own opinion about what the writers present in the *Investigations* workbook. Focus on one or two key ideas or points. Why do you agree or disagree (or both)?
b. Write about a connection that you see between your own experience and what the writers discuss in the workbook. How does it apply to you?
c. Write about how your thinking regarding economic class has changed—the new insights or understanding you've developed from the module.
d. Write about the connections you see between the current module and earlier ones.
e. Write about one (or more) parts of the workbook that are difficult for you to understand. What, as far as you are concerned, makes the material hard to understand?

These are only some of the many possibilities you can choose and are not meant to be the only possibilities.

NOTE: I do not take editing (grammar, spelling, etc.) into consideration when scoring journal responses. Still, I want your writing to meet the assigned length requirements—and to be reasonably well-organized and coherent. Label each journal entry with your name, a heading, and a date.

Note. Adapted from writing assignments developed by Guy Shebat, English faculty, Youngstown State University, for use in "Getting Ahead Learning Community, 2008–10."

Appendix G2

Community Sustainability Grid

	Individual Behaviors and Circumstances	Community Conditions	Exploitation	Political/ Economic Structures
Individual Action				
Organizational Action				
Community Action				
Policy				

Appendix G3

Personal Plan for Building Resources

Step 1: SMART Goals

Resource:				
Goal:				
Monitor for SMART standards: Check each box that meets the standards of a SMART goal. Get feedback from at least one other person that it is a SMART goal.				
☐ Specific	☐ Measurable	☐ Attainable	☐ Realistic	☐ Time-specific

Step 2: Procedural Steps

Goal (from Step 1):		
Steps	**Hidden Rules**	**Starting Date**
1.		
2.		
3.		
4.		
5.		
6.		
7.		
8.		
9.		
10.		

Step 3: Where to Go to Get Help

Step	Where to Go to Get Help
1. Support systems	1. 2. 3. 4.

Step 4: Weekly and Monthly Plan

Plan for first week

Sun	*Mon*	*Tue*	*Wed*	*Thu*	*Fri*	*Sat*

Step 4: Weekly and Monthly Plan *(continued)*

Plan for next month

Sun	*Mon*	*Tue*	*Wed*	*Thu*	*Fri*	*Sat*
Sun	*Mon*	*Tue*	*Wed*	*Thu*	*Fri*	*Sat*
Sun	*Mon*	*Tue*	*Wed*	*Thu*	*Fri*	*Sat*
Sun	*Mon*	*Tue*	*Wed*	*Thu*	*Fri*	*Sat*

Step 5: Daily 'To Do' List

Keep a daily plan or "To Do" list—on a 3x5 card.

Step 6: Back-Up Plans for Closing Back Doors

Back Doors	How to Close Them
1.	1. 2. 3.
2.	1. 2. 3.
3.	1. 2. 3.

Step 7: Establish Support Team

Sample Diagram: Personal Support for Change Mental Model

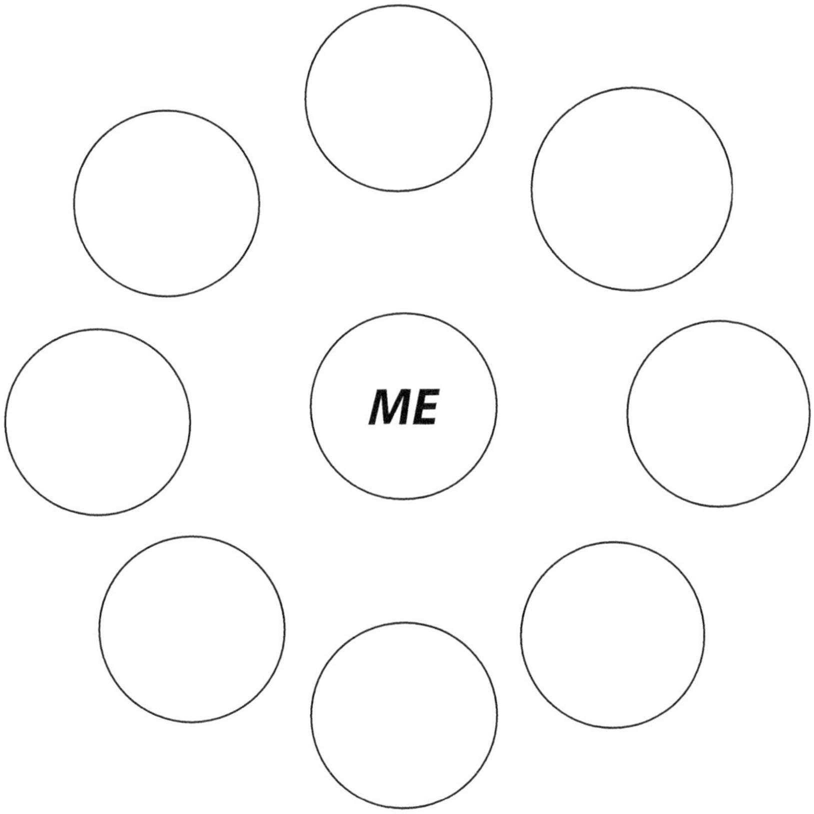

SUPPORT TEAM

Current Team Members You Want to Keep

____
____
____
____
____

People to Recruit

____
____
____
____
____

That's a plan!

Works Cited

Albelda, R., Folbre, N., & Center for Popular Economics. (1996). *The war on the poor: A defense manual.* New York, NY: The New Press.

Andreas, S., & Faulkner, C. (Eds.). (1994). NLP: *The new technology of achievement.* New York, NY: Quill.

Barkai, J. (1996). Teaching negotiation and ADR: The savvy samurai meets the devil. *Nebraska Law Review, 75,* 704–751.

Becker, K. A., Krodel, K. M., & Tucker, B. H. (2009). *Understanding and engaging under-resourced college students: A fresh look at the influence of economic class on teaching and learning in higher education.* Highlands, TX: aha! Process.

Biggs, J. B. (1986). Enhancing learning skills: The role of metacognition. In J. A. Bowden (Ed.), *Student learning: Research into practice* (pp. 131–148). Melbourne, Australia: University of Melbourne Press.

Brookfield, S. D. (1990). *The skillful teacher: On technique, trust, and responsiveness in the classroom.* San Francisco, CA: Jossey-Bass.

Brouwer, S. (1998). *Sharing the pie: A citizen's guide to wealth and power in America.* New York, NY: Henry Holt.

Brown, J. S., Collins, A., & Duguid, P. (1989). Situated cognition and the culture of learning. *Educational Researcher, 18*(1), 32–42.

Coles, W. E. (1992, November). *Keynote address.* Paper presented at Composition Coordinators' Retreat, Kent State University Regional Campus System, Newbury, OH.

Covey, S. R. (1989). *The 7 habits of highly effective people: Powerful lessons in personal change.* New York, NY: Simon & Schuster.

DeVol, P. E. (2004). *Getting ahead in a just-gettin'-by world: Building your resources for a better life* (2nd ed.). Highlands, TX: aha! Process.

DeVol, P. E. (2006). *Facilitator notes for getting ahead in a just-gettin'-by world: Building your resources for a better life.* Highlands, TX: aha! Process.

DeVol, P. E. (2010). *Bridges to sustainable communities: A systemwide, cradle-to-grave approach to ending poverty in America.* Highlands, TX: aha! Process.

DeVol, P. E., Payne, R. K., & Smith, T. D. (2006). *Bridges out of poverty: Strategies for professionals and communities workbook.* Highlands, TX: aha! Process.

Dowst, K. (1980). The epistemic approach: Writing, knowing, and learning. In T. R. Donovan & B. W. McClelland (Eds.), *Eight approaches to teaching composition* (pp. 65–85). Urbana, IL: National Council of Teachers of English.

Drill down. (2010). Retrieved from http://www.mindtools.com/pages/article/newTMC_02.htm

Fairbanks, M. (2000). Changing the mind of a nation: Elements in a process for creating prosperity. In L. E. Harrison & S. P. Huntington (Eds.), *Culture matters: How values shape human progress* (pp. 268–281). New York, NY: Basic Books.

Farson, R. (1997). *Management of the absurd: Paradoxes in leadership.* New York, NY: Touchstone.

Feuerstein, R. (1985). Structural cognitive modifiability and Native Americans. In S. Unger (Ed.), *To sing our own songs: Cognition and culture in Indian education* (pp. 21–36). New York, NY: Association on American Indian Affairs.

Freedman, J., & Combs, G. (1996). *Narrative therapy: The social construction of preferred realities.* New York, NY: Norton.

Freire, P. (1999). *Pedagogy of the oppressed.* New York, NY: Continuum.

Fussell, P. (1983). *Class: A guide through the American status system.* New York, NY: Touchstone.

Galeano, E. (1998). *Upside down: A primer for the looking-glass world.* New York, NY: Metropolitan Books.

Gans, H. J. (1995). *The war against the poor.* New York, NY: Basic Books.

Gee, J. P. (1987). What is literacy? Teaching and Learning: *The Journal of Natural Inquiry, 2*(1), 3–11.

The growing divide: Inequality and the roots of economic insecurity [Trainer manual]. (2009). Boston, MA: United for a Fair Economy.

Harrison, L. E., & Huntington, S. P. (Eds.). (2000). *Culture matters: How values shape human progress.* New York, NY: Basic Books.

Henderson, N. (1996). *Resiliency in schools: Making it happen for students and educators.* Thousand Oaks, CA: Corwin Press.

Horstman, M. (n.d.). How to give feedback. Retrieved from http://www.manager-tools.com/podcasts/Manager_Tools_Feedback_Model.pdf

Jaworski, J. (1996). *Synchronicity: The inner path of leadership.* San Francisco, CA: Berrett-Koehler.

Jenkins, L. (2004). *Permission to forget: And nine other root causes of America's frustration with education.* Milwaukee, WI: ASQ Quality Press.

Joos, M. (1967). The styles of the five clocks. In R. D. Abraham & R. C. Troike (Eds.), *Language and cultural diversity in American education* (pp. 145–149). Englewood Cliffs, NJ: Prentice Hall.

Kelly, T. L. (2004). The theme of transformation in the work of Carl Upchurch. *The new tomorrow: A voice for blacks and Latinos.* Retrieved from http://web.pdx.edu/~psu17799/upchurch.htm

Kretzmann, J. P., & McKnight, J. L. (1993). *Building communities from the inside out: A path toward finding and mobilizing a community's assets.* Chicago, IL: ACTA.

Krodel, K., Becker, K., Ingle, H., & Jakes, S. (2008). *Helping under-resourced learners succeed at the college and university level: What works, what doesn't, and why.* Retrieved from http://www.ahaprocess.com/files/HelpingURLSucceed_whitepaper05152009.pdf

Lave, J., & Wenger, E. (1991). *Situated learning: Legitimate peripheral participation.* New York, NY: Cambridge University Press.

Lobovits, D., & Prowell, J. (1996). Unexpected journey: Invitations to diversity. Retrieved from http://www.narrativeapproaches.com/narrative%20papers%20folder/journey_chart.htm

Marzano, R. J. (2007). *The art and science of teaching: A comprehensive framework for effective instruction.* Alexandria, VA: Association for Supervision and Curriculum Development.

McKnight, J. (1995). *The careless society: Community and its counterfeits.* New York, NY: Basic Books.

MGTC24: Detailed outline of weekly activities. (n.d.). Retrieved from http://www.utsc.utoronto.ca/~phanira/WebSkills/fall09-course-outline-skills.htm

Miller, W. R., & Rollnick, S. (2002). *Motivational interviewing: Preparing people for change* (2nd ed.). New York, NY: Guilford Press.

Montano-Harmon, M. R. (1991). Discourse features of written Mexican Spanish: Current research in contrastive rhetoric and its implications. *Hispania, 74*(2), 417–425.

Moustakas, C. E. (1966). *The authentic teacher: Sensitivity and awareness in the classroom.* Cambridge, MA: Howard A. Doyle.

National College Transition Network. (2009). College for adults. Retrieved from http://www.collegeforadults.org

O'Connor, A. (2001). *Poverty knowledge: Social science, social policy, and the poor in twentieth century U.S. history.* Princeton, NJ: Princeton University Press.

Palmer, P. J. (1998). *The courage to teach: Exploring the inner landscape of a teacher's life.* San Francisco, CA: Jossey-Bass.

Payne, R. K. (2005). *A framework for understanding poverty* (4th rev. ed.). Highlands, TX: aha! Process.

Payne, R. K. (2008). *Under-resourced learners: 8 strategies to boost student achievement.* Highlands, TX: aha! Process.

Payne, R. K., DeVol, P. E., & Smith, T. D. (2006). *Bridges out of poverty: Strategies for professionals and communities* (3rd rev. ed.). Highlands, TX: aha! Process.

Phillips, K. (2002). *Wealth and democracy: A political history of the American rich.* New York, NY: Broadway Books.

Pransky, J. (1998). *Modello: A story of hope for the inner city and beyond.* Cabot, VT: Northeast Health Realization Institute.

Putnam, R. D. (2000). *Bowling alone: The collapse and revival of American community.* New York, NY: Simon & Schuster.

Rose, M. (1989). *Lives on the boundary: The struggles and achievements of America's underprepared.* New York, NY: Free Press.

Sapolsky, R. M. (1998). *Why zebras don't get ulcers: An updated guide to stress, stress-related diseases, and coping.* New York, NY: W. H. Freeman.

Sawyer, D. (Anchor). (1991). True colors [Television series episode segment]. In M. Lukasiewicz (Producer), *PrimeTime Live.* New York, NY: American Broadcasting Corporation.

Senge, P. M. (1990). *The fifth discipline: The art and practice of the learning organization.* New York, NY: Currency Doubleday.

Sharron, H., & Coulter, M. (2004). *Changing children's minds: Feuerstein's revolution in the teaching of intelligence.* Highlands, TX: aha! Process.

Shaughnessy, M. P. (1977). *Errors and expectations: A guide for the teacher of basic writing.* New York, NY: Oxford University Press.

Shebat, G. (2009). *Fundamentals of college writing* [Course assignments]. Youngstown, OH: Youngstown State University.

Surowiecki, J. (2005). *The wisdom of crowds.* New York, NY: Anchor.

Tuckman, B. W. (1965). Developmental sequence in small groups. *Psychological Bulletin, 63*(6), 384–399.

Upchurch, C. (1996). *Convicted in the womb.* New York, NY: Bantam Books.

Valenzuela, C., & Addington, J. (2006a). *Four features of racism* [Available from Minnesota Collaborative Anti-Racism Initiative, 1671 Summit Ave., St. Paul, MN 55105].

Valenzuela, C., & Addington, J. (2006b). *Systemic racism: Daily strategies for survival and beyond* [Available from Minnesota Collaborative Anti-Racism Initiative, 1671 Summit Ave., St. Paul, MN 55105].

Vella, J. (2002). *Learning to listen, learning to teach: The power of dialogue in educating adults* (rev. ed.). San Francisco, CA: Jossey-Bass.

Wenger, E. (1999). *Communities of practice: Learning meaning and identity.* Cambridge, England: Cambridge University Press.

WETA-TV. (2010). Home. Retrieved from http://www.ldonline.org/index.php

Wheeler, R. S. (2008). Becoming adept at code-switching. *Educational Leadership, 65*(7), 54–58.

Wheeler, R. S., & Swords, R. (2010). *Code-switching lessons: Grammar strategies for linguistically diverse writers.* Portsmouth, NH: Heinemann.

Zull, J. (2002). *The art of changing the brain: Enriching the practice of teaching by exploring the biology of learning.* Sterling, VA: Stylus.

Index

NOTE: Page numbers in *italics* refer to display material.

M

About the Authors

Philip E. DeVol has been training and consulting on poverty issues since 1997. He is co-author of *Bridges Out of Poverty: Strategies for Professionals and Communities* (1999) with Ruby K. Payne and Terie Dreussi Smith, and in 2004 he wrote *Getting Ahead in a Just-Gettin'-By World: Building Your Resources for a Better Life* to help people in poverty investigate the impact of poverty on their communities and themselves. DeVol's 2010 work *Investigations for Economic Class in America,* co-authored with Karla M. Krodel, applies the Getting Ahead concepts to college life for under-resourced postsecondary students. A collection of DeVol's essays and articles also was published in 2010 under the title *Bridges to Sustainable Communities.*

DeVol works nationwide and internationally with communities that apply Bridges constructs, including sites in Canada, Australia, and Slovakia. In fact, *Bridges Out of Poverty* and *Getting Ahead in a Just-Gettin'-By World* have been translated into Slovak, and Bridges Communities in Slovakia have so far been awarded two European Union grants to further the work there. Bridges Communities bring together people from all classes, political persuasions, and sectors to address all causes of poverty in a systemic way. DeVol conducts quarterly phone conferences with Bridges Communities on a variety of topics to assist knowledge transfer among the many individuals, organizations, and communities that are adopting Bridges principles in their settings and developing new levels of expertise.

In addition to writing and consulting, DeVol coordinates aha! Process's collaborations with other organizations to implement innovative, high-impact strategies for ending poverty and building sustainable communities where everyone can do well.

DeVol builds on his 19 years as the director of an Ohio outpatient substance abuse treatment facility in which he designed treatment programs and collaborative systems for school-based prevention, community-based intervention, and Ohio's first alternative school for recovering young people. He resides in Marengo, Ohio, with his wife, Susan.

Karla M. Krodel is adjunct faculty in the Department of Social Work at Youngstown (Ohio) State University (YSU), teaching *Investigations into Economic Class in America* to first-generation, low-income college students. She was an early adopter of *Getting Ahead in a Just-Gettin'-By World* for college students and continues to apply *Bridges Out of Poverty* concepts in the development of model learning communities for under-resourced college students.

Krodel co-authored *Understanding and Engaging Under-Resourced College Students* in 2009 with Bethanie Tucker and Karen Becker. In 2010 Philip DeVol and Krodel co-authored the student textbook *Investigations into Economic Class in America* and the companion volume of *Facilitator Notes.* This curriculum was expressly designed to transform the educational experience of first-generation, low-income college students.

Poverty and related issues have been a constant theme in Krodel's career. Previously she supervised inpatient psychiatric units, coordinated county health department clinics, and directed a regional lead poisoning prevention program. She joined the YSU staff 15 years ago as a grant writer and served as a workforce development program director and senior research associate in the Department of Urban Studies. In her current position as director of the YSU Department of Education Outreach she creates partnerships that bring college programs to underserved populations.

Krodel holds an undergraduate nursing degree from the University of Pittsburgh, as well as a master's degree from Kent State University. She resides in Lisbon, Ohio, with her husband, Craig Paulenich.